New York Voices

New York Voices

Fourteen Portraits by Whitney Ballictt

UNIVERSITY PRESS OF MISSISSIPPI   JACKSON

www.upress.state.ms.us

The University Press of Mississippi is a member of the
Association of American University Presses.

Manufactured in the United States of America

First edition 2006

∞

Library of Congress Cataloging-in-Publication

Balliett, Whitney.
    New York voices : fourteen portraits / Whitney Balliett.—1st ed.
        p. cm.
    ISBN 1-57806–836–3 (alk. paper)
    1. Artists—New York (State)—New York—Biography. 2. Intellectuals—
New York (State)—New York—Biography. 3. Gifted persons—New York
(State)—New York—Biography. 4. New York (N.Y.)—Biography. 5. New York
(N.Y.)—Intellectual life—Miscellanea. I. Title.

    F128.25.B25   2005
    974.7′1—dc22   2005052995

British Library Cataloging-in-Publication Data available

For my love N

Note

This book deals with fourteen men and women who have enriched, complected, and glorified New York City life during the past fifty years. They include three comedians (Bob & Ray, Jackie Mason), an Americana dealer (John Gordon), a radio and film producer (Jean Bach), a harpist (Daphne Hellman), a tubist (Harvey Phillips), an entrepreneur (Julius Monk), a librarian (Lola Szladits), three nightclub owners (Max Gordon, Barney Josephson, and Bradley Cunningham), and a painter and his art historian wife (Jon Schueler and Magda Salvesen). All have tempered their skills with improvisation and even bravura. Indeed, they have made works of art out of their professions.

W. B.

Contents

New York Voices

Régisseur

JULIUS MONK

Manhattanites didn't stay home much at night fifty years ago. The streets were safe, and things were cheap. If they didn't take in a play or a movie (sometimes with its own stage show), they went night clubbing. An astonishing number of night clubs came into being in the city between the end of Prohibition, in 1933, and the fatal entrenchment of television, in the fifties. These clubs offered singers, comedians, diseuses, jazz, cocktail pianists, harpists, classical guitarists, revues, mimes, dancers, ventriloquists, puppeteers, monologuists, and harmonica players. They included the great ballrooms and dance halls (the Savoy, Roseland), glitzy pre-Las Vegas palaces (the Latin Quarter, the Copacabana), ethnic music halls (Sammy's Bowery Follies, the Lorelei), posh hotel rooms (the Persian Room, in the Plaza; the Cotillion Room, in the Pierre), jazz clubs (Minton's, Jimmy Ryan's, Kelly's Stable, the Downbeat, the Famous Door, Hickory House, Nick's, Eddie Condon's), and supper clubs (the Ruban Bleu; the Blue Angel; the Café Societys, Downtown and Uptown; In Boboli; the Little Club; Bon Soir; Spivy's Roof; One Fifth Avenue; the Downstairs; the Village Vanguard). The supper clubs were the dandies of New York night life; intimate, rarefied, even precious, they were frequented by the gentry, the nouveau riche,

3

show-biz people, and the remnants of European royalty still afloat in the city then (White Russian, Italian, Greek, Spanish).

Four men ruled the supper clubs: Herbert Jacoby, a Frenchman, who started the Ruban Bleu in 1937, modelling it on Le Bœuf sur le Toit, in Paris, and filling it at first with foreign performers, like Lotte Lenya, Marianne Oswald, Greta Keller, and Mabel Mercer (Jacoby was ahead of his time; three years later, Le Pavillon moved from the World's Fair to Manhattan, forever changing American attitudes toward food); Max Gordon, a writer manqué from Lithuania, who opened the Vanguard in 1934 and, with Jacoby, the Blue Angel in 1943; Barney Josephson, a Trenton shoe salesman of Latvian extraction, who founded Café Society Downtown in 1938 and Café Society Uptown in 1940 (the first completely desegregated night clubs in the country); and Julius Monk (no relation to Thelonious), a pedigreed North Carolinian, who took over the Ruban Bleu from Jacoby in 1942, ran it for fourteen years, started the Downstairs, and the Upstairs at the Downstairs, and finally closed his career in the late sixties at Plaza 9-, a mini-theatre fashioned out of what had been the Rendezvous Room, in the basement of the Plaza Hotel.

Relying mainly on intuition and divination, these men trained and graduated a couple of generations of singers, comedians, and actors, who went on to enliven Broadway and Hollywood and to put television and Las Vegas on their feet. Some of the members of this celebrated army: Bil and Cora Baird, Carol Burnett, Sylvia Syms, Imogene Coca, Barbra Streisand, Harry Belafonte, Aretha Franklin, Lena Horne, Jim Backus, Jack Gilford, Betty Comden and Adolph Green, Abe Burrows, Professor Irwin Corey, Zero Mostel, Judy Holliday, Orson Bean, Anita Ellis, Bobby Short, Jonathan Winters, Cy Coleman, Barbara Cook, Mort Sahl, Mike Nichols, Elaine May, Tammy Grimes, Patti Page, Wally Cox, Dorothy Loudon, Dorothy Lamour, Liberace, Tom Poston, Pearl Bailey, Andy Williams, Phyllis Diller, Eartha Kitt, Lenny Bruce, Woody Allen, and Lily Tomlin. Of course, as Max Gordon once pointed out, "there were a great many people—this is one of the sad things about show business—who performed and did nothing and disappeared."

The supper-club performers had to please their audiences and the men who hired them. But they also had to win kudos from the mysteriously powerful newspaper gossip columnists, among them Dorothy Kilgallen, Walter Winchell, Leonard Lyons, and Cholly Knickerbocker—a kind of dangerous Greek chorus, who echoed every whisper and flutter in the clubs, telling their readers who had been seen where the night before, who was (by insinuation) sleeping with whom, who was rising, who was slipping. It was a couple of the classier columnists who, in the early forties, took to calling Julius Monk—probably at his sly behest—a conférencier (lecturer) or régisseur (stage manager).

Herbert Jacoby died in the seventies and Barney Josephson and Max Gordon in the eighties. But Monk goes serenely on. Now seventy-nine, he resides in genteel, cluttered Edwardian splendor in a small aerie on West Fifty-seventh Street. He lives surrounded by mementos (a heavy brass paperweight in the shape of a heart is inscribed "To Julius a Beautiful Man a Gentle Master My Love Tammy"), photographs, watercolors (a fine one, by the composer Harvey Schmidt, of the ramshackle building that the Downstairs first occupied, on West Fifty-first Street), oils (of him, his mother, his father, and Provincetown, and an abstract landscape by Stark Young), huge hand-tooled Mark Cross scrap-books, and an Empire sleigh bed covered with needlepoint pillows, many of them sewn by his friend the singer-pianist Hubbell Pierce, and embroidered with the name of one of the revues Monk produced at the Downstairs or at Plaza 9-.

Monk is watched over closely by his longtime friend Virgil Whitney, a management consultant, who lives in Turtle Bay. "People have said that Julius is desperate for money," he said not long ago. "That is not true. He is quite comfortable, though he would be rich if he had signed a 10-percent contract with all the people he brought along. But he never operated that way. If he has been distressed about being retired, he has never let it show. He is quite stoic. It was the end of an era when he retired, and he was smart enough to recognize it. He reads. He loves to eat. He keeps in phone contact with old friends like Imogene Coca and Dorothy Loudon. He travelled extensively for a time—Mexico, London, Paris. But his arthritis makes it difficult for him to get around now, and his vision is limited. And he had some heart trouble a while ago and was told he had to lose thirty pounds, which he did. He was very upset last fall by that dreadful, vulgar book about night clubs called *Intimate* something or other. He has a large part in it, and it is full of inaccuracies and innuendo—the kind of thing that one simply does not have a way of dealing with. If he took a more cynical view of life, he would be less put upon. But he can be gullible and naïve, and that is surprising when one considers how much time he spent in the venal, narcissistic world of show business."

When he receives visitors, Julius Monk sits on a love seat in his living room, a cane held between his knees. He sits very straight and looks straight ahead. He is slightly over six feet tall ("six and a half feet," as he puts it), and his hair is white and thinning. The extraordinary dark-haired handsomeness of the Monk of thirty or forty years ago—poetic, almost smoldering good looks, like those of the young Alec Wilder or the young Orson Welles—rests just inside his high-domed, gently aging face. (Monk began modelling in the forties, and became one of the highest-paid male models in the land.) He doesn't smile very often, and, when he does, it is the memory of a smile. He still talks in stately, ceremonial rhythms. He likes to put little breaks in his words; "hiring," for instance, comes out "high-ring." His accent is unique. It has two sources—an upper-class North Carolina drawl and a kind of Oxonian, possibly picked up in the thirties, when he hobnobbed with the Duke and Duchess of Kent. (The New York gossip columnists had trouble with the royals; sometimes they had Monk hanging out with the Kents, sometimes with the Yorks.) Every second paragraph, these disparate languages lock, and an entire sentence goes by, its face turned to the wall.

His life has been divided into five parts: his rapscallion youth, which ended in 1934, when he left the Cincinnati Conservatory and moved to New York; his seesawing years, from 1935 to 1940, spent racketing endlessly back and forth between Europe and New York, an itinerant pianist and boulevardier; his tenure as the régisseur of the Ruban Bleu; the dozen years he spent as the producer of brittle, brilliant revues at the Downstairs and Plaza 9-; and his long, graceful retirement. His talk tends to move on many legs and in many directions. Here, collated (and translated when need be), are some of his recollections.

"When I came to New York after Prohibition, I got a job playing piano at the One Fifth Avenue bar. Joe Lilley, who was at the Greenwich Inn, joined me, and we became the duo of Joe and Jules. A celestial-looking girl named Dorothy Lamour sang with us for six months. She had the most sensual sound. She simply *breathed* a song like 'I'm in the Mood for Love.' She and Joe went to Hollywood, and a year or two later she starred in *The Hurricane*. This was the time of the debs. Cobina Wright had her own radio program, and there were singing contests for the débutantes at Armando's and bobbing for balloons at the Stork Club, some of them with hundred-dollar bills concealed inside. Then I met Eliza Allen. She was a sculptress who had studied with Jo Davidson, and she had come over from France to sue her ex-husband. Her father had been a major general under Black Jack Pershing, and her great chum in Paris was Katherine Anne Porter. We made pilgrimages to places like the Statue of Liberty, and we decided to get married.

It was a *mariage de raison*. When I took her home to meet Mother and Father, he never once called her Mrs. Monk. She might just as well have been an instrument of the Devil. We lived together two years, then went our own ways. We were divorced in 1942.

"I had always been determined to get to Paris by the time I was twenty-one, but I missed it by two years. Eliza and I crossed on the S.S. *Lafayette*, and I played 'Truckin'' in a tossing sea. I believe it was new then. In Paris, I played double piano with Garland Wilson at the Dingo Bar, just around the corner from the Dôme. Herbert Jacoby, who was running Le Bœuf sur le Toit, and Jimmie Daniels, who later had the Bon Soir in New York, were around, and so were Mabel Mercer and Bricktop and, a little after, Jean Sablon and Charles Trenêt and Hildegarde. In time, I became the artistic director of the Paris Ruban Bleu. Jacoby had started it. But I was drinking heavily, and 90 percent of the time there was no rhyme or reason to anything I did. I remember finding myself one night at Brick-top's, unannounced from New York, and being put to work immediately. I made a screen test, and played at Brummell's in London, after the Duke of Kent got me working papers. I became part of the group that wintered in Paris, travelled to the Riviera in the heat, and ended the summer in Salzburg and Budapest. In Budapest, everything was inundated with paprika, and there were vast orchestras with thirty or forty violins, and they sang 'Gloomy Sunday,' the suicide song."

In 1950, Dorothy Kilgallen turned over her column in the *Journal-American* to Monk for a day, and he wrote, "In the summer of 1937, we went down to St. Tropez, a fishing village in the south of France, got two pianos from Marseilles for which we were almost banished as witches by the natives who had never seen any before, rented a seventeenth-century house and opened Chez Julius, an open air terrace, where we made a killing by serving corn-on-the-cob, corned-beef hash, and hot dogs at fifteen francs a throw to such clientele as Prince Philippe of

Greece, the Duke and Duchess of Kent, and Marlene Dietrich. Peak of the season came with a contest for the most amusing sandals; judges were Marlene Dietrich and Noël Coward. A man won the prize."

Monk always seemed to know where he was going. "I was born in Spencer, North Carolina, on November 10, 1912," he said. "When I was seven, we moved to Salisbury. My father was Henry Laurence Monk, and my mother Nancy Catherine Blackwell Monk. I had an older brother, Laurence, or Henry, Jr., who was a dentist, and an older sister, Catherine, who married Bill Peacock, a correspondent for the A.P. She lives in a senior community in Alexandria, Virginia, and she's eighty-six and even flakier than I am. The other day, I called to ask her if she could remember when our parents died, and she said she'd look it up. She called back five or six hours later and said, 'What was it you called me for, Julius?' My father was a surgeon for the Southern Railway, and he had five brothers, all medicos, and, of course, that is what I was sup-posed to be. He was a handsome, balding gentleman, six and a half feet tall. He rather alarmed me and I rather alarmed him. He had a Southern overlay of Clarence Day—an autocrat at the dinner table. He always wore bespoke clothes, and that was unusual in Salisbury. He liked a kind of hopsacking with a Biltmore weave. He was quite musi-cal and played the violin until Laurence sat on it. Whenever he caught me playing popular songs on the piano, he'd close the lid and lock it. My interest in alien music made me an important sinner. My mother was born in Pelham, North Carolina. She had a distinctive walk and a magnificent carriage and the most beautiful legs and feet. She and my father both studied singing, and she had a pretty parlor voice, sweet tones. My father was Catholic—I think a great-great-uncle had been converted on his deathbed. My mother was not, and her two brothers took a dim view of her being courted by a Catholic. It was a trying courtship. My mother was bone-dry when I arrived, and I was turned over to a wet nurse, who raised me. For years, Mother was incapable of caring for me herself—she had a goitre problem and a troublesome climacteric. I was sent to St. Leo's Hall. My father's two sisters, who were nuns, taught there. There were about thirty-five boys and thirty-five bottles of Syrup of Figs on the mantelpiece. From there I went to Belmont Abbey, which was run by Benedictines.

"My mother thought early that I had artistic inclinations. She said I'd probably be a window dresser, but I didn't like that. I already had the fantasy life of the theatrically inclined—a fantasy life questing an audience. One would envision great successes without a specific vision. We had a seven-story skyscraper in Salisbury. A gentleman scaled the building, and the entire town turned out to watch. Right away, I sent off for a book on how to walk on the ceiling. This was done by fastening rubber suction cups to your shoes. I had seen trapeze artists in the circus, and when I swung on our swing I'd hang on by my knees and go so high I almost made a complete circle. I was electrified when people stopped to watch.

"I started running away when I was eight. The first time, I took a knapsack and put three sausages in it and got to the adjacent village, about four miles away, before someone asked me if I was Dr. Monk's boy. When I was fifteen and a half, Father sent me to the Peabody Conservatory, in Baltimore. Straightaway, I bought a raccoon coat and charged it to my mother and went to New York and checked in at the Piccadilly Hotel. It was the only hotel in New York I had ever heard of. I spent my days at the Capitol Theatre and lived on milk-shakes. My father alerted the Missing Persons' Bureau in New York and wrote to the New York newspaper columnist O. O. McIntyre, and I was found in the Piccadilly lobby and sent home. I mooned around when I got there, so Father sent me back to New York, to Manhattan College. After a few weeks, I was very un*galant* and said baloney to the whole thing. I packed my steamer trunk and got into a taxi and went to the Greenwich

Inn, in the Village. I thought it was an inn, but it was a night club, and it was closed tight. Someone told me that Papa Strunsky rented accommodations to starving artists, and I got a room in his building on MacDougal Street for three dollars a week. I found a job playing piano at Abe Brown's Round Table. A policeman was stationed by the door every night to make sure no one drank, and poets like John Rose Gildea and Eli Siegel declaimed. I met a woman named Eve Peri, who made tapestries and sold them to the Met, and I moved in with her on Greenwich Avenue. That adventure ended when my mother, who had come up on the Crescent, arrived at the door."

Monk began working off and on as a pianist at the New York Ruban Bleu in 1939. "Herbert Jacoby had opened the Ruban Bleu in an empty room over Theodore's Restaurant, at 4 East Fifty-sixth Street, and soon I was there three days a week and three days at the Brevoort or the Lafayette, in the Village. Jacoby and I knew each other extremely well from Paris, and most of the time we were in accord. When we scrapped, I'd take off and play at the Café Montparnasse, which later became La Vie Parisienne. I believe it's now La Grenouille. The wonderful harpist Casper Reardon was at the Ruban. He was first harpist under Eugene Goossens, of the Cincinnati Orchestra, and he could play tenths on the harp. Cy Walter and Stan Freeman played duets, and Paula Laurence was doing comedy. Jacoby left the Ruban Bleu in 1941 and, two years later, started the Blue Angel, on Fifty-fifth Street, with Max Gordon. I took over as the régisseur at the Ruban in September of 1942, and we had Maxine Sullivan, the Delta Rhythm Boys, and the harpist Ruth Berman. The room seated just a hundred and twenty-five. There was a tiny service bar, and the tables were the size of cufflinks and were covered with a kind of contact paper. The chairs were imitation nineteenth-century café chairs, and the walls were a *bleu français*. There were banquettes along three walls. We had two grand pianos, which sat side by side right on the floor, and behind the pianos was a screen on which hung two enormous sailor hats, with decorative ribbons, that had been designed by the milliner Mr. John. The female performers dressed in our little office, and the men used a mezzanine off Theodore's. The service personnel wore black tie and tails. The music, generally provided by me, began at ten, and the show went on at ten-forty. We had no microphones and no spotlights. There was a dispirited 'Star-Spangled Banner' at eleven-forty-five, and when everyone left, at curfew, it looked like a victory parade pouring into Fifth Avenue.

"I was never catastrophically wrong about the talent I hired. I discovered intuitively that some talents take time to emerge. I don't think you can ask a performer to display talent on demand. Imogene Coca was very slow. After her first night, the owner of the Ruban asked me to let her go, but I said that if she went I went. In two weeks, she was fine. After I brought Sylvia Syms in, I taught her to pay attention to the lyrics and stop trying to sound like a horn. I told her that getting the lyrics across safely is a question of manners. Some things were exceedingly difficult to deal with—singers who had vibratos that you could skip rope with, or whose tones were too sec. But I always had a surreal comprehension of comedy, of the intricate, fallible mechanism of comedic timing. There were so many intangibles—taste, pacing, obstreperous guests, mood, getting all the members of a trio or quartet to feel good at the same time."

Sylvia Syms, still going strong, spoke about Monk the other day: "He took me into the Ruban from a club on Fifty-second Street. He taught me about the verses to songs and about good songs like 'Down in the Depths' and 'True Blue Lou.' He taught me that a song has emotional peaks and valleys and how to find them. And he taught me that as a performer you don't fall in love with yourself; you fall in love with your partner—the audience. I loved the way he introduced me, in that accent of his: 'Ladies

and gentlemen. Please direct your attention and applause to our very spirited diva in the round, Miss Sylvia Syms.' And I loved to watch him bring
out the wonder in other performers. He had the most incredible gift for
zooming in on what needed to be edited in a performance, what needed
to have a tuck taken in it, what needed to be cut. Julius had a wild sense
of humor. Once, we were sitting out front in a club listening to this dippy
blonde sing. After each number, Julius would nod and give a little clap,
and when she finished he leaned over to me and said, 'My dear, what the
fuck was that?' "

In the summer of 1946, Monk visited Provincetown, on Cape Cod. "I
found Hugh Shannon banging away on the piano in this Portuguese dive,
and that got things started," he said. "Hugh and I began giving shows on
Sunday nights in an old saloon in a hotel called the Atlantic House. It was
the kind of place where travelling salesmen stayed. We appropriated two
giant uprights and painted their tops white and their bottoms blue. We
found some booths in a defunct Chinese restaurant, cut them in half, and
made them into banquettes. Hugh and I played duets, and Daphne
Hellman, who had rented Jack Phillips's house with her husband,
Geoffrey, did 'Lesson with a Harp,' which started 'First you F around.'
And Imogene Coca was with us. We could seat seventy-five, and we dis-
covered we could succeed. The following summer, we put in lights and
painted the room dark blue and green and white, and called it the Kem-
Tone Room. The ladies in the show wore gowns and the men tuxedos.
Bibi Osterwald came, and Marilyn Cantor did a chilling takeoff of Ethel
Merman. She was a daughter of the famous Cantor, so it was a brush of
grandeur. The Provincetown *Advocate* got behind us, and the genteel
Nautilus Society, and the drakes and swans began hacking down the
A House lane. The critics came from Boston, and we sold out every
night."

The Provincetown caper lasted two or three more summers. Then, in 1953, Monk was invited by some admirers from Bermuda to put together a show for a limited run at the Bermudiana Hotel. He gathered ten or eleven of his Ruban Bleu regulars, among them Jack Fletcher, Bibi Osterwald, Bill Dana, Jean Caples, and Alice Pearce, and they rehearsed at the Village Vanguard and Spivy's Roof, and took off for Bermuda. The show, *Stock in Trade*, ran for seven weeks and was a great success. It was Monk's first revue. Two years later, he left the Ruban Bleu. He described what happened next in an introduction to *Baker's Dozen*, the script of his twelfth revue, published in 1964:

> After fourteen-odd years as *régisseur* of Le Ruban Bleu, I was let out to pasture and grazed serenely for six weeks at the Hungry i in San Francisco's North Beach. Upon returning to New York, I began an association with the Playgoers—a premises at Fifty-first Street and Sixth Avenue consisting of a subterranean passage and street-level bar of riotous aspect. Good fortune permitted me to indulge my variety vagary; in the Downstairs Room, *Four Below* (in association with Murray Grand and with prudent guidance from John Heawood) was painlessly delivered. On March 4, 1956, Dody Goodman (far above par before Paar), Jack Fletcher (alumnus of Bermuda, Ruban, and Cape), Gerry Matthews (teamed with Tom Poston for Ruban debut) and June Ericson (superb soprano, also Ruban debut diva), with Murray Grand and Stan Keen's spellbinding spinets . . . extended a cordial invitation to the citizens to descend the stairs and view our wares.

Monk offered fourteen more revues during the next twelve years: *Son of Four Below, Take Five, Demi-Dozen, Seven Come Eleven, Pieces of Eight, Dressed to the Nines, Ten-ish, Anyone?, Struts and Frets* (done in Chicago to test the waters outside New York; the audiences, Monk said, "cheered us to the echo," but he never went on the road again), *Dime a Dozen,*

Baker's Dozen, Pick a Number, Four Below Strikes Back, Bits and Pieces, and his last revue, *Four-in-Hand,* given in 1963 at Plaza 9-. The shows' casts numbered from four to eight, the music was by duo pianists, and although solo, duo, and trio voices came forward, the shows were mainly ensemble efforts. Few of the actors became stars, because stars were not encouraged. (Among the best known were Ronny Graham, Dody Goodman, Ceil Cabot, Bibi Osterwald, Alice Ghostley, Tammy Grimes, Alice Pearce, Jane Connell, Mary Louise Wilson, Gerry Matthews, Ellen Hanley, and Rex Robbins.) The same was true of the shows' writers, composers, and lyricists. (But we remember Bart Howard, William Roy, Harvey Schmidt, Tom Jones, Carolyn Leigh, Portia Nelson, Stephen Sondheim, and, again, Ronny Graham.) Gilbert and Sullivan hovered over the revues. There were patter songs, playlets, monologues, and dialogues. Monk called his revues "spoofs," and they were. Their targets included politicians, singles bars, folk songs and torch songs, Timothy Leary, cigarettes, William Zeckendorf, hippies, the suburbs, highfalutin musical societies, James Bond movies, shopping bags with department-store names on them, Mary McCarthy's *The Group,* and Edward Albee's *Who's Afraid of Virginia Woolf?,* done as *Who's Afraid of I. J. Fox?* (a once famous furrier). The women performers wore black cocktail dresses or black evening gowns, and the men wore tuxedos. The shows had a fast, hide-and-seek quality. Heads and arms and gloved hands popped out of a panelled front cloth and disappeared, and the number of people onstage changed constantly. The only props were stools of various sizes.

Monk continued, "After I started the revues at the Downstairs, it became a collaboration with the choreographer and the writers and the composers. I hated being magisterial, and I suppose I was regarded as a benevolent despot. There were things I insisted on, like the performers' making eye contact with the audience. To do that, you had to guard against the lights' being too low. I also invented a different kind of front cloth. It was made of vertical panels, which enabled a performer to stick his head through and make announcements, or whatever, sort of like a puppet show. I paced the shows, and the pace was fast, although I wasn't a fan of constant motion. We always had the danger of a drinking audience; when anyone got too loud, I'd put the houselights up. For a while, we had a number about the John Birchers, which had the lines 'Mommie is a Commie, You've got to turn her in.' Birchers began showing up, and they'd raise a ruckus and try and stop the show. I did the last revues in 1968, because people were not coming. Television was closing in, and you couldn't make jokes anymore about ethnic things or the Kennedys or the upheaval all over the world. Doing the revues was a form of life I found exciting. I liked the feeling of the drawing room they had, of the Victorian supper room. I liked the nearness of the audience."

The supper clubs had begun falling by the way in the late forties. In 1948, Barney Josephson closed Café Society Uptown, forced out of business by the Hearst press, which linked him, by innuendo, to his brother Leon, an avowed Communist who had been cited for contempt by the House Un-American Activities Committee. Herbert Jacoby and Max Gordon thereupon bought the Uptown, revamped it at enormous expense, and reopened it as Le Directoire; within a year, it sank from its own luxurious weight. The Ruban Bleu closed in the fifties, and Gordon, having bought Jacoby out, sold the Blue Angel in 1964. (He had already turned the Village Vanguard into a jazz room.) Jacoby and Bobby Short started Le Caprice around the same time, but it, too, foundered. A surprising resurgence of supper clubs—or cabarets, as they began to be called—took place in the seventies. Possibly inspired by the success of Short, who had replaced the venerable cocktail pianist George Feyer in the Café Carlyle in 1968, the St. Regis reopened the Maisonette and installed Mabel Mercer in the St. Regis Room, eventually renaming it for her. The Algonquin put singers back in the Oak Room. (Greta Keller had been there in the thirties.) Michael's Pub and

Soerabaja flourished on the East Side, and Reno Sweeney, the Ballroom, and Jan Wallman's thrived in the Village. Barney Josephson, long purposely incommunicado, converted his Cookery, an elegant coffee shop on Eighth Street and University Place, into a miniature Café Society Downtown.

The renaissance subsided in the late seventies, and only the Oak Room, the Café Carlyle (still Bobby Short's pedestal), and the Ballroom survive. (They have recently been joined by Rainbow and Stars, which is now experimenting with revues.) There is a scattering of comedy clubs, where untried comics work out and pray they will be spotted by a television producer. But the handwriting remains on the wall. Live entertainment—a phrase that would have puzzled the Victorians—is slowly but steadily becoming an expensive anachronism.

Virgil Whitney, who often stops by late in the afternoon, arrived, and asked Julius Monk if he could make him a chocolate Slim-Fast, and Monk said, "Please." He went on, "In 1970, I took a job as a piano recitalist in La Boîte, just off the St. Regis lobby, but it was the wrong place for me. Then Bobby Short suggested I go into his room at the Carlyle while he was away, and I did, for five weeks. I played between five and seven-thirty, and I recall people coming in from Sotheby's and riffling through their catalogues. I haven't been able to play the piano at all for two years, because of my arthritis. I miss it. If one is unhappy, it can restore one. I had some cardiac trouble a year ago, and the medicine I take tends to make me dilatory. It is often supine time for me, and I have to take a starter pill in the morning to get my heart going properly. The fact is, the erosion of the human frame will not be denied.

"I wished, of course, to pursue my modelling career after I closed Plaza 9-. But when I answered a call for an Arthur Treacher-type person I was told they wanted a *young* Arthur Treacher, as if there ever was such a thing. I discovered that one can become de trop."

A Great Flowering of Free Spirits

JOHN GORDON

Early in the third week of every January, a short, voluble, scholarly New York dealer in Americana named John Gordon nervously loads a small hired van with an all but priceless collection of American folk art (a pair of painted Windsor chairs, a tavern table, a settle, three or four frakturs, a Pennsylvania Dutch dower chest, assorted water-colors, silhouettes, and miniatures, a pillar-and-scroll shelf clock, a dozen slipware pie plates, an Elmer Crowell carved bird, several primitive paintings, two or three quilts, some Shenandoah jugs, a bannister-back chair, a joint stool, and a Bellamy eagle), almost all of it acquired in recent months, rides with his cargo from his shop, on West Fifty-seventh Street, to the 7th Regiment Armory, at Sixty-seventh and Park, where he has been invited to exhibit at the Winter Antiques Show, a benefit for East Side House Settlement, drives in the back door of the armory, on Lexington Avenue, helplessly watches union hefties handle his cases and cartons, unpacks, sets up a small booth in one-twentieth the time he would prefer, and, for the next ten days, stands around for nine hours at a stretch (he is now and then spelled by his wife, Leah) and amiably gives the pedigree of each piece he has, watches eyebrows lift when he quotes prices, watches booted feet chip the original paint off the base of his dower chest, watches out for shoplifters, and occasionally writes out a sales slip and accepts a check from someone he has never seen before and may never see again. When the show ends, at 6 P.M. on the last Sunday of the month, he packs up what he has left, has the truck reloaded, drives back to his shop, unloads, and collapses for a week. But this rigorous dance is performed every week at antique shows all over the United States by Americana dealers, who in the past decade have doubled in number. They are the chief movers and celebrators of American folk art, which, in the making since the early 1700s, was largely unknown in its own land until well into this century.

American folk art might be said to be any functional art invented and/or practiced in a spontaneous and often solitary fashion by largely self-taught artisans, among them primitive painters, wood- and ivory-carvers, glassblowers, textile-makers, tinsmiths, blacksmiths, carpenters, potters, and cabinetmakers. The first folk-art explosion all but ended with the Industrial Revolution. It was, unavoidably, mostly the work of whites, although there are a few examples of black painters, woodcarvers, and potters and there are the pottery, rugs, jewelry, and baskets that Native Americans began producing in quantity in the last half of the nineteenth century. Because of its richness and breadth and originality, the earliest American folk art is unique in the Western world, and it helped offset the overbearing, made-in-Europe culture America imported so long and so assiduously. But the counterbalancing didn't begin until the 1880s, when this country, stirred by the centennial celebration of 1876, suddenly realized it had a past. One of the exhibits at the Centennial Exposition, in Philadelphia, was a reproduction of a "New England" log cabin of 1776, which contained Peregrine White's cradle, John Alden's desk, and a Governor John Endicott chair. America was thus hilariously out of touch with its past. Log cabins were rarely built in New England—indeed, they were a specialty of nineteenth-century settlers in other parts of the country—and the cradle and desk and chair were Pilgrim and not Revolutionary War relics. Moreover, the guides at the exhibit reportedly dwelled not on the beauties of the furniture at hand but on how its crudity and quaintness pointed up American progress. This new if awkward absorption in American history was also a reaction to such phenomena as the robber barons, urbanization, the financial panics, the dark, bullying weight of Victorian houses and trappings, and the endless press of immigrants, who, it was feared, would turn the country into a Tower of Babel, thus removing English from its role as the mother tongue. The first patriotic societies— the D.A.R. and such—were formed, and patriotism became a secular religion. Books on Colonial houses and furniture appeared, along with the first antique shops, which had evolved from roadside "second-hand" stores. In 1909, the Metropolitan Museum of Art put on the bellwether Hudson-Fulton Exhibition, which was devoted wholly to Early American furniture, painting, metalwork, and pottery. And the following year the Museum acquired the Bolles collection, the pristine major private collection of Americana. The first important explorers were already out in the field, among them Edwin Atlee Barber, a Philadelphia ceramics expert, who "discovered" Pennsylvania Dutch pottery, which had long been considered made in Europe. *Antiques*, the handsome, corseted doyenne of the profession, began publication in 1922, and two years later the Robert de Forests opened the American Wing of the Metropolitan. By the end of the decade, such pioneer restorations as John D. Rockefeller, Jr.'s, Williamsburg and Henry Ford's Wayside Inn were under way, and they were followed, during the next twenty years, by Old Sturbridge Village, Old Deerfield, and Shelburne. These were mostly the inspirations of wealthy, foresighted visionaries who at the same time were amassing folk-art collections that amounted to private museums. (They even had their own curators.) Then, in the early sixties, the country, as sorely perplexed by internal upheavals as it had been in the late nineteenth century, suffered its second great attack of nostalgia. The first symptom was the campy fascination with comic books, Orphan Annie mugs, old movies, and recordings of big bands and radio programs. The Museum of American Folk Art opened in New York. New restoration projects were begun, including Doris Duke's renovation of much of Colonial Newport, and more and more preservation societies, with Ada Louise Huxtable on bugle, went at it hand to hand with greedy real-estate developers. A flood of books on Americana appeared, and Americana dealers came to the fore in a field where they had long been regarded as country bumpkins.

Once the pastime of scattered antiquarians, the selling of antiques has now become a full-time business. There are at least fifteen thousand dealers in the country, and there are hundreds of antique shows, many of them run by little cartels that do nothing else. These shows range from the glacéed East Side House show to flea markets, which specialize in Niagara Falls memorabilia and the wicker porch furniture of the teens and the twenties, and which flourish on Sundays in supermarket parking lots. Very little of this has anything to do with real antiques. The definition of an antique has blurred in recent years. One hundred years has long been the rule of thumb, but today sixty-year-old Tiffany glass and thirty-year-old toy soldiers command handsome prices. Only so many good ladder-back chairs and decorated stoneware crocks were made, and the supply, because of attrition and increasing demand, constantly diminishes. So chicanery is rife (and so, too, is thievery; rarely does an issue of *Antiques* go by without several cries for help from burgled collections), and there are fake old glass, fake old weathervanes, fake old theorems (stencilled paintings or watercolors done on velvet or paper by genteel housebound girls in the nineteenth century), fake frakturs (brilliantly colored birth, baptismal, or marriage certificates, whose ornate script and wild watercolor renditions of symbolic flowers, animals, and hearts were the work of Pennsylvania Dutch artists in the eighteenth and nineteenth centuries), fake old furniture, fake old pewter, fake old ironware, and fake primitive painting. What are admittedly reproductions, sold in their own emporia, are on hand at prices often exceeding those of the objects on which they are modelled, and one can find elegant copies of Chippendale chairs as well as fair imitations of toleware — exquisite hand-painted tinware produced in the nineteenth century in Pennsylvania, New York State, Ohio, and New England.

Fewer than a hundred first-rate antique dealers occupy a pantheon above this maelstrom, and a dozen of them work exclusively with Americana. The latter are a rare breed. They are one-man bands who must be scholars, aesthetes, salesmen, accountants, indefatigable travellers, buyers, appraisers, and undercover agents. And when they are informed by one of their spies, or "pickers," of the existence, three hundred miles away, of a fine previously unknown Ammi Phillips portrait, they must be on the doorstep the next morning, cash in pocket and sporting an indifferent manner. (Pickers are odd, often highly skilled ghosts who, unequipped for the rigors of nine-to-five living, pass their days scouting for good stuff in the perpetual twilight of attics, barns, cellars, and the parlors of ancient recluses.) They must also be able to see beauty and value in objects that have hitherto been ignored. (Good toleware coffeepots sold for fifty dollars five or six years ago; one recently went at auction for over fourteen hundred.) Most important, they must, in a rapacious and seductive arena, where prices have doubled and tripled in the last couple of years, remain morally impregnable.

John Gordon is singular even among Americana dealers. He is one of the very few first-rate folk-art dealers based in a major city, the majority of Americana dealers being bucolics who set up shop in the country, where overheads are low and where they feel close to their source of supply. He has been in business not quite eight years, but his knowledge and the extraordinary quality of his stock are such that he is consulted by restoration projects, auction galleries, and museums, the last of which also buy from him. His clientele includes both the glamorous (Rockefellers, Vladimir Horowitz, Andy Warhol, Katharine Hepburn) and the unknown, some of whom are wealthy and some of whom buy on the cuff. He does not make himself easily available. He exhibits in only one show a year—the East Side House—and he runs his business almost singlehanded; if he is out of town, as he often is, his shop is closed. (His wife, Leah, has now gone on a part-time basis at *Time*, where she has worked for eleven years, and she helps him out several days a week. Gordon, in fact, has recently changed his trade name from John Gordon to Leah and John Gordon. He is also on the verge of closing his present shop, and in March, after a month's vacation, he will reopen in more spacious quarters on Fifty-seventh Street, between Fifth and Sixth Avenues.) The shop, on a second floor between Eighth and Ninth Avenues, is difficult to find, yet it is almost never empty, and there are generally a couple of clients who have stepped off planes from Montgomery or Chicago an hour or two before. Gordon has little sympathy with the distracted bohemian look of most folk-art dealers. He is neat and compact, and he wears out-of-fashion spectacles, closely trimmed hair, and an immaculate Vandyke, which sharpens the heartlike outline of his face. His eyes are deep-set and shrewd, and he has a surprisingly big voice and a confident, easy laugh. Although he moves quickly, chin up, like a small Chris-Craft, he has an eighteenth-century sense of time, for he is an impassioned, oracular Ancient Mariner who will sit in his shop and discourse on the beauties around him for hours at a time. It is impossible to drop in on Gordon for fifteen minutes; one sets aside at least two hours, which are invariably capped by a twenty-minute, standing-in-the-doorway farewell.

Gordon's shop is in a narrow, six-story apartment building, and it occupies a long room that looks south through murky windows onto Fifty-seventh Street. Several small rooms open off it, and until three years ago, when he secured the back apartment on the same floor, he and his wife lived in the shop. It generally includes half a dozen painted and unpainted Windsor chairs, several pairs of primitive portraits (their often middle-aged subjects bearing the patient, yoked look of people accustomed to cold rooms and a heavy Jehovah), several frakturs, a pale-red tavern table, a statuesque, grained Palladian-back side chair, shelves of slipware plates and redware jugs, a Pennsylvania Dutch dower chest (its colors soft, humming yellows and blues), two or three weathervanes, a red toleware coffeepot and a black toleware will box, three or four brilliantly colored Pennsylvania Dutch quilts, a stolid, knee-high black wooden horse (probably carved for a child), a seaman's chest with a crooked frigate brightly painted on the inside of its lid, a pair of sea-green metal wall sconces, a huge figurehead of a woman, her nose flattened by waves and weather, a tabletop covered with lacy, abstract butter molds, and two tall chalkware dogs with painted, rheumy snouts.

It is a recent late morning, and Gordon sits in a small Windsor chair in his shop. He talks about some frakturs he has just seen. "Taste is not absolute. It is always changing, always creating a fresh sense of rightness. A genuine piece must speak to you of a particular time and place. It must speak to you of its purposes and motivations. If it doesn't, there is something wrong with it. Eight pieces of fraktur were already on display for a New York auction when the auctioneers became suspicious and asked me to examine them. You examine such things aesthetically at first, then you look at them academically. They looked very real, very attractive, very neat. But after a while I became uneasy. Although they were in different styles and were supposedly from different periods, I had the peculiar impression that they were done by the same person. Several things put me off. The size and proportions of the paper were wrong, and each piece had a sharp center fold, as if it had been taken from an old book. I went out to lunch; I wanted a fresh eye. When I came back, I discovered that the script was brownish fading to purple. But old ink doesn't fade in that way. It bites into the paper. Sometimes it bites right through the paper. Then I examined the writing and the images, and I was convinced. In the time of frakturs not many people could write, and the men who did the script on frakturs were learned professionals. They wrote in a natural way, but someone trying to duplicate that naturalness would inevitably express *himself.* He'd either become sloppy or stiff. He would never capture the natural flow of the real fraktur artist. Also, the images on either side of each fraktur matched too closely. If the pedestal of a vase was slightly off on the left side, it was on the right as well, and the same with the facing birds and tulips. In a genuine fraktur, the facing images are almost always dissimilar, no matter how slightly. I went home and thought about it for a day and then passed on my suspicions to the auctioneers. The frakturs never appeared at the auction."

When he smokes, Gordon waves his cigarette like a baton, regulating the dynamics of his words. He likes to startle his listeners by frequently and abruptly changing the subject. "To some people, the term 'provincial furniture' is unappetizing. They prefer 'country furniture.' But 'provincial' is better if you think of it in terms of the provinces, of pieces made, say, in Worcester or Lancaster—places that did not have the great wealth in the eighteenth century of Newport and New York and Boston and Philadelphia, where high-style furniture flourished.

High-style furniture—Queen Anne, Chippendale, Hepplewhite—and provincial furniture are diametrically opposite. High-style furniture was generally made of hard woods, like walnut and mahogany, and there tends to be very little distress in such woods, which is why so many high-style pieces are in almost pristine condition. Also, their owners were well-to-do and had servants who took exquisite care of their pieces. But provincial furniture was made of local woods, often soft woods. Hickory or ash bent easily for arms, and seats were carved from pine or poplar. Provincial pieces were often painted, and for two reasons—for decoration and to disguise the different grains of the woods used. This camouflage also helped preserve the wood. The colors were far brighter than we think. We forget the patina, the mellowness that age gives paint. Many of the deep greens we see now were gaudy greens, many of the grayish blacks were true black. And the paints were often homemade. Red was pulverized brick mixed with buttermilk, which was a natural adhesive. But the great appeal of a good provincial piece is its revelation of the life it has led. It takes on its own character with use. The effect of the human body on the chair shows—the way an arm is worn, the way a seat changes, the way a stretcher is rubbed flat by generations of feet. The reason for collecting such furniture is not nostalgic. There's no point trying to escape into the past. The past was just as difficult. But the pain involved in everyday living now is mitigated by having things around you that have grace and warmth and depth. Collectors are criticized for relishing material things rather than spiritual things. This may be true of the collectors of bottle caps and matchbox covers, and it may be true of the fanatical one-track collectors of, say, a certain kind of chair or quilt. Those are self-contained manias. But in acquiring American folk art you are consciously or unconsciously attempting to alter reality around you. You are surrounding yourself with the results of a great flowering of free spirits, of democracy *really* at work. It took an amalgam of people from the world over to cause this flowering, which became a flowing continuum of folk artists—not peasant artists, because there were no peasants here—who carved things and glazed things according to the dictates of the wood and the clay and their great taste. But it was not vanity expressed in wood or pottery. Everything made was functional. A weathervane showed the direction of the wind. A small carved wooden lion was a child's toy. A toleware pot held coffee. And a scrimshaw tooth reminded a sailor's girl that he was thinking of her five thousand miles away. But these functional, everyday things were beautiful as well. That weathervane pointed into the wind *and* enriched the sky, that wooden lion roared, that coffeepot, with its reds and yellows and greens, glowed and danced. Their makers desired to alter *their* reality because of the inherent need in people to lift and purify their environment, and in so doing lift and purify themselves. And, of course, their art did not come out of a mainstream. It didn't evolve directly from the work of predecessors, as European peasant art did. Nor was it stifled and trammelled by the things that existed in Europe, like an oppressive aristocracy and guilds and academies, which snuffed out originality. It was spontaneous in its time and place. Grandma Moses, despite her occasional sweetness and cuteness, was a good example. She had no consciousness of the existence of 'art.' Her spontaneity and individuality is obvious. Take an English Windsor chair. It sits there with this stolid, here-I-am-to-stay look, this forever-England look. It is anchored to the earth. But a great American Windsor takes off and goes into flight."

The antique business, like any specialized, introverted endeavor, has its own argot. This is especially true of furniture. Some examples:

Turning: The shaping of wood into a series of symmetrical circular knobs. Done on a lathe or by hand, often with turning chisels.

CREST or RAIL: The horizontal piece of wood, carved in an endless variety of shapes, that tops the back of a chair.

SPINDLE: One of the spokes of wood that form the back and that support the arms of a Windsor chair.

STRETCHER: One of the horizontal spokes, often turned, that are fastened between chair legs for support.

EAR: A decorative carving at each end of a crest made in the form of an abstract human ear.

ONION FOOT: An onion-shaped piece of wood on which a chest rests.

REEDING: A continuous narrow groove, used to decorate the edges of furniture.

KNUCKLED END: The end of a chair arm carved to resemble knuckles.

SPLAT: The vertical backrest of a chair, often carved in vaselike shapes. Flat or slightly curved.

CABRIOLE LEG: A furniture leg carved in a flattened S-shape. Its contours are almost a caricature of the human leg from the top of the calf to the ankle.

Gordon points to an unpainted comb-back Windsor armchair. It has a spidery grace. "Consider this American Windsor. Without doubt, it's an exquisite object. In the realm of Windsors, it's a high accomplishment. It's one of a kind, to begin with; there is no other chair precisely like it. And that's thrilling. In early America, there was very little room or time for nonsense. So there's nothing in the chair that shouldn't be there, except a little embellishment—the pieces of jewelry that bring out the sparkle in your lady's eye. The chair is light in weight, and the way it is put together is a challenge even to American creativity. It has no nails, no screws, no glue. There's a seat, four legs, some stretchers, some spindles, and a single, shaped arm, and they are all held together by the maker's understanding of wood. He wet the pieces before he assembled them, and when they had dried the *exact* amount of time, he put them together. Just enough contraction took place, and the chair's members are still gripping each other two hundred years later. The chair has subtle turnings. They are fully realized but not overly voluptuous. It has a continuous arm that was steamed into its curve, and there are delicate knuckled ends. The crest undulates quietly and has sculptured ears. There is a handsomely shaped saddle seat. Its legs and the spindles supporting the arm have an excellent rake, which gives the whole a spirited, jaunty look. Note that the arm and the seat are reeded. A distinguished touch. And the icing on the cake is that the chair is signed on the underside of the seat. It says, 'Made by D. B. Austin for his cousin Daisy Olive Berry.' Then there is a punched design of entwined hearts, and 'To my sweetheart.' I don't know who Austin was or who Daisy Berry was. But that chair is a very personal statement. It was the brilliant effort of one person in one particular place working at the top of his knowledge and wits."

A well-tailored, somewhat dour middle-aged couple arrive at the shop. They are from the South and they come to New York once a year, and they always make an appointment to see Gordon. They have the intense, preoccupied expression of collectors out to buy. They look at pottery and chairs. Gordon talks quietly but assertively, slipping into the editorial "we" that Americana dealers often adopt at work. It has an impressive, corporate ring, as if each opinion and fact he is expressing were being tacitly echoed by a legion of watching, equally expert dealers. Gordon sells simply by dwelling lovingly and eloquently and exhaustively on each object examined. The couple decide on a large piece of signed Shenandoah pottery, its dark browns and reds swirling smokily around its sides. And they choose a pair of handsome, matching unpainted Queen Anne side chairs with gracefully curved splats and fine cabriole legs. Their passion spent, the couple immediately surface and become cheerful. Gordon makes out a bill and closes the transaction with a joke. "Amazing! It comes to exactly seventeen hundred and seventy-five dollars. I'm tempted to add a dollar." He laughs, and the husband laughs and sits down and writes a check. The couple leave, after a fifteen-minute round of goodbyes. They have been there an hour and forty minutes.

"It is astonishing how you find things," he says. "Most of the process is mundane, but some of it is very exciting. People call you and you receive pictures in the mail. You get to know collectors, and perhaps one of them, out of the need for money or because he is getting old and has no heirs, starts selling off his collection. I am buying an entire collection right now, bit by bit, from a man in New Jersey. He has been collecting for fifty years, and, with one or two exceptions, when he was fooled, he has beautiful things. The prices he paid are often still marked on the bottom of pieces, and they make you weep. Like that pierced-tin lantern over there. It's a beauty, and he got it for five dollars. A good, reasonable going price now is a hundred and ten. But your most important source is generally pickers. They're strange, dedicated people who are in love with the field, and they come in all varieties—poor, rich, uneducated, educated. I have a picker, a fantastic man, whom I can buy from sight unseen because he has such perfect judgment and taste. A picker from New Jersey, who was also a painter, told me about one of the most impressive things I've ever owned. It's a weathervane, and it's now in the Newark Museum. It's a cock with spurs, and it has a huge beak of a nose and an extraordinarily detailed cutout tail. It's four or five feet across and was made from a single sheet of iron, which is exceptional. It's in superb condition, and I'd guess it dates from about 1700. It was owned, the picker said, by a rather unstable woman. In fact, she was a drinker. He took me out to see her. She lived alone in a hovel, and the weathervane was in her barn. It had been made for a nearby Dutch Reformed church, and she had gotten it from her father. He had been a handyman who worked for the church and had helped take the weathervane down some fifty years before, when the elders decided it might fall off and kill someone. Her father put it away in the barn, and it was forgotten. I asked her what she wanted for it, and she told me, and I said, 'Fine.' Then, I don't know whether she took a dislike to my glasses or what, but suddenly she said, 'No, you can't have it.' I was terrified, but I played it cool, and said that I understood she might feel too attached to it to part with it, and we left. A year later, she relented, and I got it. I brought it here and hid it in a closet because I was so overwhelmed, but one day a close friend of the Newark Museum stopped by and the closet door was open and he said, 'My God, what's that?' and that was it. Other things are handed to you on a platter. One summer evening, fifteen or so years ago, I went to an auction at the Plaza Art Galleries, on East Seventy-ninth Street, and afterward I decided to walk home. Not far up the street, I looked in the window of a little shop called Bernal Antiquary. It's gone now, but it was typical of its New York kind—filled with bits of armor and marble statues and European ceramics. I looked a little, then I spotted a wall cabinet, about two feet square, with a door and iron hinges. It was sitting by itself on the floor at the back of the shop. I couldn't believe my eyes. It *looked* like a classic eighteenth-century Pennsylvania Dutch hanging wall cupboard. I went in and tried to be calm. I still wasn't a pro, and I was afraid I might muff it. Finally, I asked the owner about it. He said, 'Oh, God, that thing! That's been here for years. I'm sick of it. I'll sell it for thirty-five dollars. No, listen. I'm so sick of it I'll give it to you for thirty dollars.' I told him not to bother wrapping it and ran out hugging it and screamed for a cab. I discovered I was right when I got home. It was beautiful, wholly original, and very rare. It had a double raised panel in the door, marvellous rattail hinges, and exquisite details in the wood. It was a tremendous find, and the astonishing thing was that it had sat there so many years near an auction gallery that every dealer in the country visits at one time or another. It's hanging in my living room, and I'll never sell it, and even if I did I have no idea what I'd ask—eight, maybe ten thousand; I don't know. It's priceless. That's one end of the spectrum, but I've been to the other, too. Just after I went into business, I got a letter from a woman in Maine, saying that she had seen a picture in the *Times* magazine section of a cigarstore Indian I had. She said she had one just like it, and that she was interested in selling. I wrote back and asked her if she had a picture of it, and she said no, but the Indian was really worthwhile. I finally went up there, and the minute I arrived I smelled a rat. Her house was full of schlock. I didn't see the Indian, and she said it was in their summerhouse. Back into the car and to the summerhouse, which was dark and empty, save for a monstrous round pedestal table with snakes coiled around its base. I asked her where the Indian was, and she pointed to a corner, and there it was. It was about two feet high. I tapped it. It was made of plaster and was the sort of thing you win in a carnival booth by hitting bull's-eyes. And so you learn. You also learn about the occupational hazards of being on the road so much. Another time in Maine I was going inland to see a picker. Leah was with me. I was on a two-lane road, and I was going about fifty-five. It was a ten-day trip, and we'd been travelling all week. I momentarily dozed, and I lost it. The shoulder of the road was soft, and down we went. Leah screamed. There was a tree, and the tree didn't move. Half my head went through the windshield, and I broke my arm. My wallet somehow ended up out in a field. Leah was all right, but she was wearing a seat belt and I wasn't. The worst thing, I had several sheet-iron weathervanes in the car. We could have been beheaded. We were taken to a hospital, and the doctor on duty was Mexican. He was extraordinary. For hours, he picked glass out of me. But we didn't stay overnight. We left as soon as he was finished. We had to, or else I don't think I would have stepped into a car again. We even antiqued on the way home, and it was a way to celebrate being alive."

Gordon locks up the shop and walks quickly down the hall to the back apartment to get lunch. He eats a corned beef sandwich and then brews some tea. The telephone rings, and he talks for twenty minutes with a man in Maryland whom he has never met but who calls him every week and buys sight unseen. He sits down with a mug of tea and talks of his upbringing in Philadelphia, where he was born in 1921. "My father, who recently passed away, was a concert violinist, and he became a furniture-maker and an upholsterer when he developed arthritis. He lived in a house there that I own, and he was always a quiet, unassuming man, albeit an enterprising and resourceful one. I did not have the closeness with him that I had with my mother, who died five years ago. But then he was not close to anyone. My mother was shy but friendly and not at all aggressive, but she was the one who set the standards. We had a deep understanding and I could always turn to her for sharing and discussion. Her father had been a Polish rabbi—a poor man but a typical devoted scholar. And she had a brother who was a mural painter in Poland and had studied in Paris. Eventually, he worked for the Czar and settled in Tashkent, where he surrounded himself with orchards and oranges and bolts of silk. He wanted my mother to settle in Tashkent, but she was afraid of pogroms. The revolution came. My uncle had become a member of the élite, and we never heard from him again. I had three sisters—one older and two younger. One passed away when she was sixteen, and none of us could get over it. Her passing haunted me, just as my mother's still does. My mother was the last member on her side of the family, and there was a great finality about it. But I often wonder why it is inconceivable that you will not again meet those very meaningful to you in some gentle eternity.

"I got a sixteen-hundred-dollar scholarship when I graduated from high school, and I went to the Philadelphia Museum College of Art. I studied advertising design three years there, and I took painting courses at night. It was a balance between art and commerce I have tried to maintain all my life. When I was twenty, I volunteered for the Army and went into the Signal Corps, which was inscrutable to me. I also got married the first time, and I think getting married was as frightening as the thought of being killed. I had never been away from home except for the summer of 1939, which I spent in New York with an aunt and uncle. It was a memorable summer. I got interested in the art scene, I went to the World's Fair, and I heard Gershwin played at Lewisohn Stadium and wept along with everyone else. After the Army, where I ended up painting murals in Army buildings for a marvellous Southern colonel named Rosenberg, I went to the Pennsylvania Academy of Art on the G.I. Bill. I spent the whole of one summer painting around Rockport and Gloucester. It was the only time I have painted and done nothing else. I took a job with N. W. Ayer in Philadelphia in the fall of 1944, and I was with them two years. There was no money in it, but it was a civilized place, and I won an award for a box I designed for facial tissues called Yes. And, along with a lot of the other people in the art department, I painted furiously at night. I think we painted more at night than most full-time painters. Then I enrolled in the Art Students League, in New York. It was a robust period in art in New York—Pollock and de Kooning and Rothko and Miró and Chagall and Lipschitz. I got to know Rothko, and I met Pollock. He was a wild man. He was introverted and couldn't mix, and he was always loaded. He gave the impression his shoes were always too tight. Then back to Philadelphia and to the Philadelphia Museum. It was not an anti-Semitic place; there was simply no history of Jews' making it there. And it was run by dollar-a-year men—a kind of private club that depended entirely on contributions from well-to-do Main Liners. At the same time, I enrolled at the Barnes Foundation, and came under the sway of old Barnes himself, who was irascible and brilliant. It was through visiting his country place that I first became exposed to Pennsylvania Dutch folk art, which he had been collecting since the thirties.

"In 1951, my wife and I moved to New York. I still had some of my G.I. Bill, so I studied art history at N.Y.U. for a year. Then I went with McGraw-Hill. I was there eleven years, and eventually became an art director. The last six years, I worked a lot at home, and, although I had been collecting folk art for a good many years, I became genuinely serious about it. I even began selling on the side, and my first client was a lady who was donating a room to the Cincinnati Museum. A dealer had sent her to me. I wish I still had the things I sold her. One was a flat, wrought-iron fish, about ten inches long, and you'd swear it was made in this century by someone like Brancusi. It was meticulous in design and detail, and it was the epitome of American functional folk art, for it was an axehead holder that was fastened to the side of a Conestoga wagon. I sold it for thirty-five dollars, because I was so excited at selling something that would be in a museum. I've discovered since that there are only three known to exist. She also bought some beautiful miniature slipware plates and a New England wrought-iron finial depicting St. George killing a dragon.

"Then my wife and I got divorced. Leah and I were married, and it was time for a new venture. I had always considered the antique dealer's way of life with envy. And I now felt prepared to handle it. I had no fear of not being able to get good things, and no fear of not being able to judge things quickly and safely, which a dealer must do. It was no longer just the occasional piece you're buying for your own pleasure. My interests and acquaintances were broad enough so that I had good contacts. There were gaps in my knowledge. I didn't know scrimshaw, but I do now. There didn't seem to be anyone on the scene who handled things the way I had in mind, and I felt the time was generally ripe. I sensed a new and dynamic interest in Americana. The Folk Art Museum had just opened, and Americana dealers like Jim Abbe, in Oyster Bay, were going strong. Things happened quickly. I exhibited in the Thirty-fourth Street Armory show in the spring of 1965, and I had marvellous stuff, like a red toleware gooseneck teapot with a big yellow bird as a motif. It went for a ridiculous price. It would bring thousands now. In fact, with the prices I was charging, you could have bought the entire contents of my booth for a couple of thousand, and I would have been wiped out. I remember a certain New York folk-art dealer going through the booth from top to bottom and not buying a thing. But I guess no one had any eyes at that show. I opened the shop on April 13, and I did the fall show at the armory, where I had another smashing booth, with things like an iron weathervane that had a witch riding a broomstick and chasing a bat. The managers of the East Side House show spotted me there and invited me to exhibit the following January, and I'd only been going six months. It's the only show I exhibit in now. My turnover is steady in the shop, and I don't think any other show would help me. And shows are overbearing and exhausting and costly, to say nothing of the backbiting and internecine warfare that goes on between dealers. But it's amazing. I don't have any more *cash* now than I had seven years ago. I never take anything on consignment—many dealers do—and most of the money I make goes right back into stock. There are very few rich folk-art dealers."

Gordon gets up and goes into the living room. He turns on several lamps made out of stoneware jugs, and the room is breathtaking. It is dominated by two pieces—a large, square deep-brown Windsor chair with sumptuous turnings and a flying, akimbo rake to its legs, and a chandelier, four feet across, with twelve curved wire arms, each holding a candle at its outer end and each surmounted by a small, flat sheet-metal turkey that revolves when the candles are lit. Along one wall is a yellow arrowback bench, and crouching on it is a life-size wooden dog that is about to smile or jump, or both. A side table in front of the bench has miraculous spindly turned legs, a rural scene painted on its top, and flowered sides. Across the room is a slightly faded dower chest, its front decorated with a forest of peacocks, leopards, harts, parrots, and fish. A tall, regal pottery whippet is seated beside it. A plain old sponge-rubber sofa is at the far end of the room, and serving as a coffee table is a small, exquisitely proportioned butterfly table. Next to the sofa sits a walnut provincial chest that just misses being high-style, and on top of it is a huge chalkware cat. More chalkware fills a set of blue hanging shelves, and catercornered to them is the Pennsylvania Dutch hanging cupboard. Another set of shelves holds carved wooden objects, one of them a black man with hat in hand and a ferocious, mock-servile expression. The windowsills are crowded with toleware coffeepots and trays and redware pottery, and there is a superb punched-tin coffeepot on a low painted stool by the kitchen door. There are frakturs on the walls, and a small, delectable mirror with a crest made of intertwined hollowed-out hearts.

Gordon sits down next to the dog on the arrowback bench and pats it. "He speaks to me, he plays with me. This is largely a Pennsylvania room as it might have been a hundred and eighty years ago. I sit in here and breathe after I have been out in the city, and it restores me. I bring things in here and live with them, and if they live well they never leave. If they don't, I move them out front. This room is redolent of the two greatest folk-art dealers I have known — Hattie Brunner and Joe Kindig. Hattie was my mentor in many ways. She's in her eighties now, and she still lives in Reinholds, Pennsylvania. She started when she was sixteen, with her mother, who was one of the many early second-hand-furniture dealers. Some of the most joyously memorable days I have spent were with Hattie Brunner. I'd go out from Philadelphia by bus on a nice warm summer day. Everything always seemed lush, and there was a quietude. You felt God had been there just before you. We would have a lunch of fried oysters and scrapple and homebaked pie, and a drink of cool water from her pump in the back yard. And there were always Dutch pretzels. We would schmoose all afternoon, with her talking in that funny, high Pennsylvania Dutch voice: 'Dat's gute,' or 'Dat's humbug.' But she was never tutorial. She expressed her knowledge in a general way, and I drenched it up. Nobody knows Pennsylvania pottery better than Hattie, and it was from her that I learned how to distinguish between the various counties and makers. She could look at a piece of pottery and tell you exactly where it was made, when it was made, and who made it. Even when she had cataracts, she could judge a piece simply by holding it in her hand and feeling it. And she knew as much about fabrics and carvings and furniture and ironware. Her love and understanding of American ironware and fraktur rubbed off permanently on me. She dealt with dignity out of her own house. Sometimes two hundred people came — in fact, they still come — on Saturdays and Sundays, trooping through all her rooms, just so they could say they had been to Hattie Brunner's. And she was lovely to all of them. She built whole collections for some people, and famous collectors, like the Garbisches, came to her. Hattie knew everyone in the county, and she knew every house and what was in it. She taught me that you cannot learn by looking through a glass case in a museum. You have to be *close* to a piece—if possible, hold it in your hands, rub it, smell it, look, look, look. Hattie will live forever. I don't know how many fine pieces have passed through my hands from all over the country that have her pencil markings, her code, somewhere on them.

"The other great dealer, Joe Kindig, had a shop on the main street in York, Pennsylvania. He never washed the windows and he never swept the place. You had to wipe off the glass on his frakturs with your handkerchief before you could see them. He was lean and tall and wore his hair to his waist, and he had a yellowish-white beard. He never wore a tie and he never wore socks. He drove a yellow Cadillac and he was a vegetarian. I think he must always have had money. But he bought low and sold high, and he never lowered his prices. In fact, they always climbed. When I first went to his place, years ago, he had a fraktur that really knocked me out. It was a hundred dollars, but I didn't have the money, and Joe wouldn't come down. He'd say, 'Don't worry about money. These things are precious. They are works of art, and they will get scarcer and scarcer.' Every time I went back, the fraktur was there, but it was always just beyond my reach. He finally sold it to someone else, seven or eight years ago, for sixteen hundred dollars. Very few people hit it off with Joe, because of his seignorial ways. But he was convinced there were a chosen few, and he either recognized you as one of them or he didn't. A couple of years ago, mutual friends told me he was sick and withering away and that of course he wouldn't see a doctor. I went to see him and found him a little embarrassed at being in bed. But it was business as usual, and we talked for an hour and a half, and then he sold me that whippet. He had always refused to part with it before. I paid him, and he gave me the usual 5 percent off for paying in cash, and took his wallet out from under his pillow and made change. The last thing he said to me was 'There's something wrong between me and God, Jack, and I've got to go and straighten it out.' He died that night.

"Naturally, there are bad dealers, too. One of the worst was in Connecticut. He was fat and Germanic, and he kept the shades pulled in his house and used seven-watt bulbs. All his stock was hidden upstairs under beds. 'Hannah!' he'd shout to his wife. 'Bring down dat chug from under der second bed.' He'd declare bankruptcy, but all his goods were in his wife's name. He had a black heart and no friends. And he was anti-Semitic. Even though he had very good stuff, he cheated everybody, including me and other dealers I know. The last time I was there, I bought a fraktur and a lovely fantail rooster similar to the ones that still come out of the Tyrol. The next morning, I examined them in the sunlight at my motel window. The rooster had some new paint on it, and the fraktur had been touched up. I took them back and told him this was the end, and to give me my money back. He did, and all he said was 'Ah, Jack. You too damn schmart.' "

Gordon has been staring through the living-room door off and on at a painting hung in the kitchen above the refrigerator. It is a rural winter scene, with several buildings, done in brilliant blues and reds and oranges. A snow-covered road, with a couple of wagons on it, bisects the painting, and the road is lined with straggling toothpick fences. The daring colors balance each other admirably against the blue-white snow, and the buildings are arranged so that they seem to hang in air. Gordon goes into the kitchen and brings the painting into the living room.

"For years, I had been on the lookout for the work of a true contemporary primitive painter, and, by God, I finally found one—Harry F. Long, or shorty Long, as he was called. This is his work. I found him in a strange way. I had heard about a painter in the heart of the Pennsylvania Dutch country, and I went to see him. He wasn't very good; he was copying magazine photographs. He said he had a

brother down the road who also painted but that he wasn't as good.
What the hell, I thought, I'll go see him. It was Harry Long. I was
astonished. He had a startling and original sense of color, his trees
were living, breathing presences, and he had a great clarity and sense
about space, and what to do about space is a painter's greatest problem. I bought a couple of his paintings. The second time I went, he
had changed, improved. The fact that a city man had bought some of
his work had imbued him with extraordinary confidence. The third
time, he had built himself a little studio. He was a carpenter by trade,
and he had taken up painting at the age of sixty-six, after a heart attack.
He wore a carpenter's apron when he painted, and his palette was a
board with bottle caps nailed upside down on it. I kept buying paintings, but it was difficult to know how to handle the situation. I didn't
want him to think of himself as a discovered artist, because it might
make him self-conscious. And I didn't want to be at all critical, because
it might puncture him. The only thing I did was to take a walk with
him one day out into the country and talk to him about the sky. The sky
befuddled him; he gave it almost no expression in his paintings. I
pointed out to him how the sky constantly changes—that it might be
blue one day and white the next and gray the next. But he never solved
the problem. What interested him, probably because of his trade, were
buildings and their details. He painted the cloister at Ephrata—a
nearby seventeenth-century religious enclave that has been restored—
at least six times. And it is totally, stunningly different in each painting. Of course, he did not paint by sight but from memory. All the
Ephrata paintings were based on visits made thirty or forty years
before. And a marvellous foreshortened picture of a French village
street was what he remembered of France from the First World War.
Near the end of his life, I'd suggest subjects that he might have seen,
like an Amish wedding or a quilting bee, and he'd say yes, he had seen

them, and was interested. But then he died. He'd only been painting six years. I have almost everything he did—some fifty pictures. One mark of his great honesty and dedication was that when I asked him why he didn't paint more pictures—the more he painted the better he got—he said that painting was the most exhausting thing he had ever done, that when he finished a new picture he was worn out. In time, I suppose, I'll give a show of his paintings. Foolishly, I sold several of them for practically nothing the first year I was in business, and they were snapped up like hot cakes. Long was unique in this day. Except for the First War, he never travelled. He never went to the movies and he never looked at television. I don't think he even read magazines. He travelled in his head among the visions of what he had seen in the area he lived in all his life. He travelled up and down the fields and woods and roads of his past. He knew little about painting and nothing about art. What he did was spontaneous and private and absolutely pure."

Their Own Gravity

BOB AND RAY

During the past twenty-seven years, two smart, unassuming, strangely gifted New Englanders, born Robert Brackett Elliott and Raymond Walter Goulding, but long known in every swinging American household as Bob and Ray, have—as an amazing and unflagging repertory team—invented, fleshed out, and shepherded through the uncertain realms of radio, television, and the theatre a unique company of comic characters who bear names like T. Wilson Messy, Wally Ballou, Calvin L. Hoogevin, Wolfman, the Worst Person in the World, Webley Webster, Artie Schermerhorn, Chester Hasbrouck Frisbie, and Mary McGoon, and who are in large part gentle but hilarious takeoffs of every kind of phony, dimwit, wiseapple, bully, bore, bungler, crook, and creep. Like many inspired inventions, the creation of this magic company was accidental. The time was 1946 and the place the Boston radio station WHDH, where the two men, who had never met and had just returned from the war, were staff announcers. Bob had a morning record show and Ray gave the hourly news reports. In the manner of Sissle and Blake, Gilbert and Sullivan, Laurel and Hardy, and Ellington and Strayhorn, they discovered almost immediately that they had a telepathic bond they still don't fully understand. They speak of the same "wavelength" and the same "chemistry." They mention such coincidences as having the same birth month (a year apart), losing one or both of their parents when they were eighteen, and being raised near Boston. But after that, they look out the window and lapse into puzzled silence. This lightning mutual understanding soon led to on-the-air badinage, generally following the newscasts, and then to the invention of their first comic figures: Wally Ballou, a bumbling reporter whose voice was based on the sound of an adenoidal New England janitor at the station; Mary McGoon, who gave recipes and menus in a dreamy falsetto and was patterned on Mary Margaret McBride; and Charles the Poet, who, the prototype of every bad high-school English teacher, read sentimental verse to organ accompaniment, and, after a stanza or two, burst into uncontrollable laughter. Both men had long been addicted to radio (just as the young are now addicted to the movies), and their idols included such early radio figures as Stoopnagle and Budd; Billy Jones and Ernie Hare, the Happiness Boys; Fred Allen; "Vic and Sade"; and Raymond Knight, who populated two programs, *The KUKU Hour* and *Wheatenaville*, with funny imaginary figures. They also admired Laurel and Hardy, whom they somewhat resemble physically, and it is not an exaggeration to say that their roots, whether or not they are conscious of it, even go back to the hyperbolic madness of Dickens, whence so much twentieth-century humor comes. They parodied inarticulate sportscasters, pompous newscasters, rambling culinary experts, soap operas, dramatic shows (their *Mr. Trace, Keener Than Most Persons* was a takeoff of *Mr. Keen, Tracer of Lost Persons*), and such oddities as *The Answer Man*. The ingenuity and variety of old-time radio has long since been replaced by three monolithic formats—news, music, and talk—so the source of much of their original material has vanished. (They are hard at work these days, though, on those radio shows built around know-it-all emcees who argue with and even insult telephone callers and, most recently, on television talk shows.) But a miraculous thing has happened to their comic company; instead of falling by the wayside, since parody generally exists only as long as its original does, it has taken on a life of its own and exists completely within itself, its occasional topical forays notwithstanding. Its once parasitic humor has become organic and self-renewing. The countless young people who have discovered Bob and Ray in the past six months—the two men returned to radio early in March, after an eight-year absence, and can be heard every afternoon on WOR from three-fifteen until seven—have never heard the old soap opera *Mary Noble, Backstage Wife*, upon which their daily adventure *Mary Backstayge, Noble Wife* was at first based. That isn't necessary. *Mary Backstayge* has its own laws (or non-laws), energy, motivations, and atmosphere; it is an independent comic-surrealist world. And much the same is true of the rest of their world, for it is now clear that their original parody went much further than radio: it was aimed—and still is—at plain human foolishness.

Radio is a curious medium. It is like trying to watch a play through an opaque scrim or a movie when the projector lamp fails. It renders our eyes useless while it agitates the mind's eye. In its way, it is an electronic form of the great Victorian pastime of reading aloud. Bob and Ray, forbidden the props of visual humor on radio, have made an art of comic aural effects. To be sure, they have been visible off and on, during their career on television, in the theatre, and in a single movie, and they are good visual comedians. But radio is their habitat. Freed from concern over what to do with their arms and legs and faces, they can develop to the fullest the marvellous non-stop music of voices at the heart of their work—a music that is continually buttressed by myriad sound effects: explosions, footsteps, Bronx cheers, closing doors, sounds of fighting, laughter, applause, sounds of eating, and so on, many of which they once did live themselves but all of which are now on cassettes, played

at the right moment by the studio engineer. Ray, who has a deep baritone, handles both the low and the falsetto voices. The gradations in
each register are subtle and infinite. He uses deep, guttural tones that
often explode into terrifying roars (for Captain Wolf Larsen, a remarkable creation made up of elements of the hero of Jack London's *The
Sea-Wolf*, Long John Silver, and Dr. Jekyll and Mr. Hyde), a leaden voice
(for bores), a light, husky voice (for lunatic pedants), a brisk, matter-of-
fact baritone, close to his own voice (for manipulators), a heavy, toothless voice, which he achieves by tucking in his upper and lower lips
and gumming it (for Calvin Hoogevin, a character in *Mary Backstayge*,
and for Webley Webster, whose main function is hanging around the
studio and occasionally playing "Jalousie" on the "huge WOR pipe
organ"), a flaying, grating baritone (for Commissioner Carstairs, who
was introduced into *Mary Backstayge* during the Army-McCarthy hear-
ings, in 1954, and sounded like a dead ringer for McCarthy), and, at
the opposite end of his vocal spectrum, a number of falsettos, varied
by subtle rhythmic displacements (for all the Bob-and-Ray females).
Bob has a pleasant light baritone. He, too, is a good mimic, and has at
hand Peter Lorre and various French, English, and German accents.
He also has an adenoidal, pinched-nose voice (for Wally Ballou and
Pop Beloved, another figure in *Mary Backstayge*), a light, floating,
almost diaphanous drunk's voice (for Kent Lyle Birdley, an old-time
radio announcer who gives genteel household hints—"Don't take hot
food out of your mouth with your fork; sip some water instead to cool
the mouth"—and drinks his way through two-and-a-half-hour
lunches), and a flat, dull voice (mainly for Harry Backstayge, Mary's
slow-witted husband). But there is more to their humor than these
ingenious flutings. Along with parody and their special, rackety brand
of surrealism, they use slapstick, sheer nonsense (the McBeebee
twins, who talk in fugue form), topical humor (Wally Ballou has until

the other day been running for mayor of New York, and his campaign headquarters, in a room on the ground floor of the WOR building, were closed not long ago for a couple of days while they were debugged), arcane references to old-time radio (Dismal Seepage, Ohio, mentioned not long ago on *Mary Backstayge*, was borrowed from *Vic and Sade*), hyperbole, non sequitur, and surprise. They have faultless timing, and they are effortless. Dick Cavett has said, "They're immaculate performers. They're like the finest actors: there's simply too much to absorb completely in any one sequence. They have none of that sketch-playing broadness a lot of comedians fall into, and they never, never let on that they're trying to be funny. They are certainly as great as Nichols and May." Alec Wilder, the composer and acute freewheeling critic, has studied them even more closely. "In a curious way," he says, "they are sociologists who are on the edge of being critics. By means of hyperbole, they manage the effect of defining levels of society, of cant, of pretension. They are—if there is such a word—catharsisists. They produce their own gravity, as in Newton, and they turn it off and on as they choose."

Though they are so close in spirit, philosophy, and wit, Bob and Ray are almost totally dissimilar in appearance and manner. Bob is trim and of medium stature. He has a small mouth, aquiline features, and receding, sandy-reddish hair. He dresses with verve and precision. He is introverted and speculative and quiet-voiced, and his shy, slightly pop-eyed look suggests an honorably retired Scottish colonel who has recurrent nightmares about being drummed out of the regiment. Ray is as impervious as a mountain. He stands six foot two and has ample girth. Double chins, a generous nose, and smoking black eyebrows dominate his face. His voice booms and caroms. He has an easy sense of dress, and will sally forth in a pair of light-blue pin-striped trousers, a purple shirt, and a gray seersucker jacket. He laughs a lot, and he walks with rapid, earth-gobbling strides. Extrovert winds seem to encircle him, giving him an openness that continually leads strangers to seek him out. Old ladies ask him floorwalker questions in department stores, and in bars he is taken for an Irish cop. The differences between the two men can be epitomized thus: When their Broadway show, *Bob and Ray: The Two and Only*, opened, in 1970, they received only one bad review—a wet-fingered tirade from John Simon. Bob framed it in silver and hung it at home, which is in the East Sixties; Ray has never read it. But the two men share one physical characteristic. Like most old-line broadcasters, they are indefatigable throat-clearers, and when they are in the same room the ceaseless coughs, harrumphs, and roars are almost deafening.

Few humorists are given to exhaustive autobiography, and Bob and Ray are no exception. When they are interviewed in their offices on Lexington Avenue, they have a cautious, preoccupied air. "I was born in Boston in March 1923," Bob said late one morning. "But I grew up in Winchester, a suburb north of the city, near Melrose. I was an only child, and so was my mother. She came from Maine, and was quite artistic. Whatever artistic talents I have—I paint watercolors and make furniture and such—came mostly from her. She did needlework and refinished old furniture and painted tôleware trays. She had an uncle who was typical of her stock: he ran a drugstore in a town of four hundred people in Maine for sixty-five years. Before he died, he gave me the soda fountain in the store, and it's a beauty. I have it in a house I have in Casco Bay. My father was an insurance man and a native of Cambridge. He was a good father, and I had great love for him, but he died when I was eighteen. He was the opposite of me. He played piano and was musical and was very unmechanical. He couldn't pound the proverbial nail in straight. I was hooked by radio when I was very young. Whenever I came to New York with my parents, we'd go to radio shows—Ben Bernie and Rudy Vallee and Raymond Knight's *KUKU Hour*. He played a character named Ambrose J. Weems, who ran an imaginary radio station and made comments on the week's events, and he had a sidekick called Mrs. Pennyfeather, who was played by an ex-Shakespearean actress, Adelina Thomason. He also did a show, *Wheatenaville*, in which he was a small-town newspaper editor. He was a funny man and an early influence on me, and eventually he became a close friend. He worked for Ray and me as a writer in the early fifties, when we first came to New York, and after he died, I married his widow, Lee. She had two daughters, whom I adopted and who are married now, and we have three children, all still at home.

"After high school, I went to the Feagin dramatic school, in New York. It's gone now, but I think it was considered better than the American Academy of Dramatic Arts. I went in two spurts—during a summer and then for a year. Jeff Chandler and John Lund and Angela Lansbury were in my class. I worked nights as an usher at Radio City Music Hall, and later as a page at NBC, along with Gordon MacRae. Then I went back to Boston, and on the spur of the moment, in the summer of 1941, got a job as an announcer at HDH." (Radio people have the offhandedness of all communications pros, and they like to drop the first letter of a station's call letters.) "I did everything, including remotes from places in Boston like the Silver Dollar Grill and the Seven Seas Café, where they had the big black bands. Then my father died, and I was deferred from the draft until 1943. I was in basic training with an armored company, but when I was sent overseas with the 26th Infantry Division I was transferred to Special Services. Almost the entire armored company was wiped out. I went back to HDH in 1946, and Ray was hired just after. I did a morning record show and he did the news, so we ran the station from six until nine. We found out almost instantly that we were on the same wavelength, and after the news we'd bat back and forth a little. The station got the rights to broadcast the Braves and Red Sox games, and they asked us to do a twenty-five-minute show before each game. It was called *Matinée with Bob and Ray*. They had to have that rhyme, and it's the only reason we're Bob and Ray and not Ray and Bob. We started inventing our characters, and I think our first soap-opera takeoff was *Linda Lovely*. We also got in the habit of not using a script and of ad-libbing everything. In 1951 we had a chance, through Ray's older brother Phil, who was with WMGM, in New York, to sub for him and Morey Amsterdam on their weekly show, *Gloom Dodgers*. Our stint was recorded and became a sort of audition, and when John Moses, who was with the booking outfit GAC, heard it, he took it to NBC, where he had connections, and we were hired for a daily fifteen-minute show, which ran from quarter to six to six in the evening. We gave HDH a week's notice and took off. They didn't *really* believe we were leaving, and told everyone that sure enough we'd be back come fall. But things were really humming here by then. In addition to our little evening show, we had a two-and-a-half-hour morning show and a half-hour evening show, and in November we started an evening fifteen-minute television show. By then, we needed some writing help, and Ray Knight had been assigned to us. It was just about the only time we haven't done all our own stuff. The big-gun critic then was John Crosby, on the *Trib*, and if he gave you a good write-up you were in. He did and we were. The chronology of what we've done since is a little foggy in my head, but I think it goes something like this: In 1953, we went over to ABC, where we had a fifteen-minute evening TV show, and the year after that we started our six-to-ten morning radio show at INS. Peter Roberts, who's at OR now, was at INS—in fact, he'd come over from NBC with us—and it was there that we recorded that fantastic laugh of his, the one we still use behind a silly record. We were at INS until '56. By that time, we had started doing live spots on the weekend show *Monitor*, and those lasted off and on for eight or nine years. We also had an afternoon radio show at Mutual, on OR, and on top of that we started the Bert-and-Harry beer commercials for Piel's on TV. They were the stroke of Ed Graham, who was at Young & Rubicam. He came with us, and we set up the little company we have and called it Goulding-Elliott-Graham. Ed's not with us now, so the Graham has been replaced by Greybar. Around this time, we also put together an animated-film outfit, which did takeoffs of classic books and bad movies and the like, but the whole thing got so cumbersome and the payroll so long that we got out of it. We were ahead of our time is all, because it wasn't long afterward that *The Flintstones* hit it big on TV. The Piel's commercials lasted until '63, and the year before that we went on HN for an evening show, which ended in '65. In '66 and '67, we were on the *Today* show once a week, and then we began appearing on the *Tonight* show. All the while, we did slews of commercials. Joseph Levine—Joseph I., not Joseph E.— had been after us for six or seven years to do a Broadway show, and finally, in 1970, we did. Frankly, when he first approached us, we were afraid, but by 1970 we had more age, more bravery. It took six months to put the show together, and it was a great experience. The best review we got was in a Yiddish paper, so neither of us has ever read it, and the only bad one was that one by John Simon, in *New York* magazine. The show ran on Broadway six months, and then we took it on the road, playing places like Toronto, Philadelphia, Ford's Theatre, in Washington, D.C., Princeton, Stanford, and Fort Lauderdale. Lauderdale was unbelievable. The matinée audiences were all blue-haired ladies, and they didn't have the faintest idea what we were doing. They'd sit on their hands awhile and then get up and leave. They'd leave by the side exits, and one of them would hold the door while two or three others worked their way out, and meantime the theatre would be flooded with sunlight, just about destroying everything we were trying to do onstage.

"Ray and I have never had any big differences, any major disagreements. We only see each other occasionally socially, but our families are on good terms. We all went to Hawaii once, and another time we went to Gloucester, Mass. Our teaming up has been a profitable thing. We've always been able to exist. I don't know what the hell I'd do for a living if the partnership broke up. Maybe move to Maine and be a full-time painter. One thing, I'd never go back to radio announcing, even if I could get a job."

Ray arrived, just off the short train ride from Plandome Manor, on Long Island, where he has lived since he came to New York. (The two men have always lived at least twenty miles apart, Bob preferring the city and Ray the country. And they have another habit: When they work, Bob invariably sits on Ray's right. He does on the WOR show, he did on the old WINS show, and he does in their offices. Asked about this, all Ray said was "If that's true, it must be Bob's hangup. I'd sit on his right anytime.") Sleep was still visibly rolling off him. He sat down at his desk and opened a small milk carton and drank from it. Bob went into the recording room and put a couple of 78 rpms on a tape for the broadcast that day. One was a vocal by the late James Barton, who gets progressively drunker-sounding on the record and becomes all but unintelligible. It is called "Floating Down the Old Green River," and Bob said they would introduce it on the show and say that it was being sung by a friend of Kent Lyle Birdley. Ray put his feet on his desk and thunderously cleared his throat. Bob echoed him in the next room.

"I was born in March of 1922, in Lowell, Mass," Ray boomed. "My father was the overseer of dyeing and finishing in a textile mill. He was a pleasant sort of man, and my idol. He was always up on every-thing. He had the first self-starter in the neighborhood and the first radio. He'd put it out on the porch so the neighbors could listen to it. My mother was a great mimic and a great cook. There were no lumps in *her* mashed potatoes. One of my older brothers, Phil, died when he was just thirty-nine, and another one lives in Franklin Square, Long Island. My oldest sister died a year ago, and I have a younger sister in Flushing. Phil got me my first job in radio—on LLH, in Lowell. I was seventeen, and probably the youngest announcer in radio. In those days you did everything yourself. You rewrote the front page of the *Globe* for your news and the sports page for your sports. You were your own editor, you made your own transcriptions, you carried your own equipment to remotes, like the Lowell High School football games, and in particular the Lowell-Lawrence game, on Thanksgiving Day. High-school football was very big in Massachusetts then. When I was eighteen going on nineteen, my parents died, within five months of one another, and I moved in with my oldest sister. I got a job at EEI, in Boston, and a year later went into the service. I went to OCS, in Texas, and spent the rest of the war in Fort Knox. I hated the Army, and to make it livable I'd drive over to Louisville on weekends and work at a radio station there. I was married in 1945, to a Springfield, Ohio, girl—Mary Elizabeth Leader. We have six kids. I went to HDH after the war. I did the news during Bob's record show, and I began staying in the studio and bailing him out with some chatter, what with all the awful records he had to play.

"Most of our characters come straight out of our lives. Take Kent Lyle Birdley, the old-time announcer. Lately he's taken to drink. He has long, late lunches and spends most of his time across the street from the studio at a place we call the Times Square Tap. We gave him three names, so he'd have some stature. We got the idea from a list of names we saw once on a plaque—names like Ralph Moody Lancaster. Another three-namer we have is Dean Archer Armstead. He's the farm editor you used to hear early in the morning on New England radio, quoting hog prices and talking about crops and weather. Dean Archer broadcasts from the Lackawanna Field Station. Still another three-namer is Chester Hasbrouck Frisbie. He writes *Mary Backstayge*, and he has this deep, slow, measured way of talking. He discusses coming episodes of *Mary Backstayge* with us as if he were talking about Proust or Joyce. Then we have Barry Campbell. He's an old-time, hard-luck bandleader who has an all-girl orchestra."

Ray cleared his throat, swung his feet to the floor, and went into the recording room. Bob then suggested that they put the Worst Person in the World back in *Mary Backstayge*. (The W. P. in the W. never speaks; instead, he makes continuous soup-slurping and crunching sounds. He is, from all implications, an ogreish and threatening figure.) This colloquy followed:

> RAY: Hey, yeah.
> BOB: But make him John Simon, and we'll put him on the bus.
> RAY: Returning to New York from reviewing *Westchester Furioso* in Seattle.
> BOB: And use the soup-slurping and crunching sounds.
> RAY: That's right. Sitting there on the bus and making all these disgusting sounds next to Calvin Hoogevin.
> BOB: Let me see if I can dig out the cassette with all those sounds.

The results of this exchange occurred a few days later in *Mary Backstayge*, which Bob and Ray do live and off the top of their heads every day at four-twenty; it is replayed on tape at five-twenty and six-twenty. But first some background on the extraordinary tortoise-paced odyssey of the Backstayges that preceded Simon's appearance.

The principal characters in *Mary Backstayge* are Mary and Harry Backstayge, a muddled Lunt-and-Fontanne acting team in an age-less middle age; Calvin L. Hoogevin, their next-door neighbor in

Skunkhaven, Long Island, where they live; Pop Beloved, a retired stage-doorman; Gregg Marlowe, who is invariably identified as "young playwright, secretly in love with Mary"; Fielding Backstayge, invariably identified as Harry's "long-lost black-sheep brother"; and his Cockney sidekick, Eddie. Harry, Mary, Gregg, Calvin, and Pop take off by train to Seattle, for the opening atop the Space Needle of Gregg's new play, *Westchester Furioso,* in which Harry and Mary are starring. Disorder, which is a guiding force in *Mary Backstayge,* sets in at once. Mary and Gregg have adjoining compartments on the Broadway Limited, while Harry ends up in another Pullman and Calvin and Pop rough it in coach. A bully provokes a fight in a night club in Chicago, and they all go to jail. They are released, after pleading nolo contendere, and entrain on the Hummingbird Special, somehow leaving Gregg behind—an oversight that is never explained. (Loose ends are a staple in *Mary Backstayge.*) Fielding and Eddie appear several days later, hold up the train, and steal a frequently mentioned cheap brooch Mary is wearing. (Mary's brooch is still another arcane Bob-and-Ray reference to a once common radio practice. A piece of jewelry worn by a soap-opera character would be mentioned over and over during the show, finally taking on a kind of reality in listeners' minds. They would write in to ask if a copy of the brooch, or whatever, was available, and if the requests were heavy enough a piece of jewelry would be run off by the sponsor and made available at a low cost. It was a reasonably accurate way, in the days before instant polls, to judge the size of a program's audience.) A character who makes only strange African ululating sounds and is known as The Train Buff is shot in the shoulder by Fielding when he comes to Mary's aid, and Fielding is arrested. The trip resumes, and the rest of them finally reach Seattle, only to get stuck in the elevator in the Space Needle. Gregg reappears and rescues them. Rehearsals begin, and during a scene in which Mary and Harry are playing Ping-Pong, Harry sprains his ankle and Pop Beloved takes his place. He, in turn, sprains an ankle and lands in the hospital, where he is put in a room in the maternity ward with The Train Buff. Pop gets out of the hospital in three days, but his bill comes to three thousand dollars. Meanwhile, the play goes on, and Fielding and Eddie, working out of their nearby mountain hideaway, try to blow up Mary and Harry by putting explosives—called "juice"—in a bouquet of flowers Harry hands Mary onstage. Wealthy Jacobus Pike—the "Wealthy" is used as a given name—arrives from New York and, being the play's sole backer, tells the cast that with the way things have been going they are closing and returning to New York by bus. The bus is decrepit and breaks down. They are put on another bus, and the Simon episode takes place:

(*Violin music*)

ANNOUNCER (*Word Carr, done in Bob's stately voice*): Next, *Mary Backstayge, Noble Wife*, the story of America's favorite family of the footlights and of their fight for security and happiness against the concrete heart of Broadway. (*Music up and then under*) Today we join Mary, Pop, Calvin, Harry, and Gregg Marlowe on the bus that has just left Seattle, a few minutes after yesterday's episode, and we hear Mary say:

MARY (*Ray's falsetto*): Well, it seems to be going much better than that first bus we were on.

HARRY (*Bob, in a solemn voice, close to his own*): Yes, this is much smoother and much more comfortable. The engine sounds much more reliable, too.

CALVIN (*Ray, doing his toothless voice*): More scenic, too, this route, isn't it?

HARRY: Yes, I think that first driver started out the wrong way anyway. (*Loud collective laughter, coming from about twenty feet away*)

CALVIN: Ah, who's the group of people in the back of the bus? They keep passing around a paper bag and they all take a swig out of it.

HARRY: I don't know. They got on the bus just before we did. They were here when we got on. They're having a good time, all right.

MARY (*sharp-toned*): Well, they seem to be having more fun than we are, I'll say that.

HARRY: Yes, and there across the aisle is John Simon. He's got his (*terrific crunching and chewing sounds*) in a paper bag. Look at the way he goes into a sandwich. Isn't that awful?

MARY (*shocked*): Right through the waxed paper and all.

HARRY: Must be hungry, I guess. (*Crunching continues.*)

MARY: He seems like he's always hungry. I can't *bear* to watch him. I'm going to turn my back.

At two-fifteen, Bob and Ray walked over to WOR, at Fortieth and Broadway. The studio, with its windowless, baffled walls and heavy doors, had the "blind" feeling of all radio studios. Ray took off his coat and loosened his shoelaces. Bob chose the sound effects they would need that day from a bookcase full of cassettes and gave them to Ronnie Harper, the engineer. During the fifteen-minute three-o'clock newscast, the two men sat side by side before their microphones at a big, U-shaped table and shuffled through a pile of typewritten pages—improvised material that had been recorded and transcribed during the years they have been together. At three-fifteen, after a stertorous round of throat-clearings, they were off. Their show, which is sandwiched in between commercials, newscasts, weather reports, sportscasts, traffic reports, the time, and such, all of which takes up well over half the total air time, went like this:

Wally Ballou (Bob, adenoidal) appeared, and he and Ray (his own voice) discussed the debugging of his campaign headquarters downstairs. A funny vocal recording, "The Gourmet Serenade," followed. Bob (his own voice) interviewed someone who purported to be a member of their studio audience (Ray, in his light, smart-aleck voice) and who claimed that he was a troll and lived under the George Washington Bridge. Mary McGoon appeared with some popovers she had just made. Ray went into a commercial, and Mary McGoon vanished.

The Gathering Dusk, another Bob-and-Ray serial, came next. It is done every now and then, and each episode is complete within itself:

> (*Gloomy organ music*)
>
> ANNOUNCER (*Bob, in his straight announcer voice*): And now the Whippet Motor Car Company, observing the forty-fifth anniversary of its disappearance, brings you another episode of *The Gathering Dusk*, the heartwarming story of a girl who's found unhappiness by leaving no stone unturned in her efforts to locate it. (*Music up and under.*) As we look in on the Bessinger household today, Edna is resting on the Ping-Pong table in the recreation room. It's late afternoon, and Dr. Nodel, the village eye, ear, nose, and throat specialist, is just arriving.
>
> EDNA (*Ray's falsetto*): Oh, it's you, village-eye-ear-nose-and-throat-specialist-Nodel (*the words jammed together as if they were all one*). It was kind of you to rush right over and make a house call, even though I realize it's going to set me back a minimum of fifteen clams.
>
> DR. NODEL (*Bob, in a mushy, false-teeth voice*): Well, when serious illness strikes, I don't think we should let the cost of the cure become a primary consideration, Miss Bessinger.
>
> EDNA: Of course that's easy for you to say when I'm the one who's shelling out the cabbage. Every year my tax man marvels at the way my medical deductions run so far ahead of my gross income.
>
> DR. NODEL: Well, of course it's true medical costs have gone up recently, but most of the patients have solved the problem by taking out health insurance.
>
> EDNA: Well, I've dickered with a few companies about doing that myself, but I always feel too peaked to go have the physical checkup they

require before they'll issue a policy. And of course none of them offer health insurance to cover the cost of getting in shape to go take the physical to get health insurance.

DR. NODEL: I'm not sure just exactly what it was you said there, Miss Bessinger, but in any event, if you're too weak to go apply for a policy, I can see how you might be regarded as a bad risk.

The molasseslike conversation continues, and finally Dr. Nodel gets Edna to tell him why he was summoned:

EDNA: I've just been scared out of my wits all day because I seem to have lost my hearing. In fact, I feel as if my eardrums are worn to a frazzle from trying to make out what you've been saying.

DR. NODEL: Well, frankly, Ma'am, I'm surprised you've been able to hear me at all. Heavy-duty earmuffs like the ones you have on generally deaden all sound.

EDNA: Oh, my stars and garters! I completely forgot I was wearing them, village-eye-ear-nose-and-throat-specialist-Nodel. I'll bet they've been causing this condition ever since I bundled up this morning to let the cat out. Well, you just can't imagine how relieved I feel to know that I'm no longer standing in—the gathering dusk.

Some typical Bob-and-Ray nonsense erupts:

(*Music up and under*)

ANNOUNCER: Can it be that Edna's newfound sense of hearing will at last become the turning point in her struggle against misfortune?

WEBLEY WEBSTER (*Ray, his lips tucked in and gumming it*): Hi, Bob and Ray. How's the— Oh, I'm sorry.

ANNOUNCER: Will her realization that the cat has been outside all day with its earmuffs off while she's been inside with hers on only lead to further heartbreak? Join us for the next exciting episode, when Edna finds herself face to face with a frostbitten kitten in *The Gathering Dusk*.

WEBLEY WEBSTER: Sorry about that.

BOB (*in his own voice*): All right, Web. I just wanted to finish that off. I like to neaten things up, you know.

Webley Webster gave a brief report of what was going on at the Times Square Tap, and then the voice of Akbar Mytai came on. He is a character in another Bob-and-Ray soap opera, *Wayside Doctor*, which has been dormant since they returned to radio, and he is done in Bob's Peter Lorre voice. He said he was out of work and was looking for Chester Hasbrouck Frisbie in the hope that Frisbie would have something for him in *Mary Backstayge*. Webley Webster said that Frisbie was at the Times Square Tap and that he and Mytai would go and look for him. Vaughn Monroe's old theme song, "Racing with the Moon," followed, complete with Peter Robert's taped laughter. Then Bob took a telephone call:

MME. SONIA (*Ray, in a brisk falsetto*): Hello?

BOB. (*in his announcer's voice*): Can I have your name, please?

MME. SONIA: Yes, my name is Mme. Sonia, and I live in Brooklyn, and I'm a first-time caller.

BOB: I don't care whether you're a first-time caller!

MME. SONIA: Well, I'm so excited because I've been calling every day and I just get a busy signal.

BOB: O.K. What opinion did you call to state this afternoon?

MME. SONIA: My opinion is that I should get a free plug on the air for the palmistry readings I give in the dimly lit parlor of my home at 4738 East Blodgett Way.

BOB: No, I'm sorry. That's out of the question. We have a sales department that takes care of that.

MME. SONIA: Well, I only charge two bucks a throw, and I foretell the future and give advice to the lovelorn and predict stock-market trends and all like that. My readings are well worth the money, but I can't afford to advertise them on the radio the way I'd like to.

BOB: Well, you just spent forty-two seconds advertising them on the radio, and it's going to cost you, oh, maybe sixty dollars, whether you can afford it or not. I see the light flashing on our other phone. I'm going to take another call. You'll be getting a bill from us, Ma'am, and don't forget it.

Wally Ballou followed with a remote from Upper Darby, Pennsylvania, where he interviewed the head of the Freemex Watch Company (Ray, using his smart-aleck voice), which was about to put an electric wristwatch on the market. It would have an eight-foot cord and be plugged into the wall, and would prove so impractical that sales of regular Freemex watches would double. Bob and Ray talked about the redecorating of their studio and when the wine taps in the wall and the gold-leaf ceiling would be finished. Ray said what a beautiful view of Broadway they had out of their studio picture window. They talked about Henry Gladstone, an impeccable, longtime WOR newscaster who came out of WNAC, in Boston, along with Henry Morgan and Ed Herlihy, and revealed that he wears a smock when he broadcasts and keeps a finger bowl beside his microphone. Kent Lyle Birdley (Bob, in his soft drunken voice, punctuated with barely audible hiccups) talked about his two-and-a-half-hour lunch and said he had just seen Akbar Mytai deep in conversation with Chester Hasbrouck Frisbie at the Times Square Tap. Then came *Mary Backstayge*. The moment it started, Bob and Ray seemed to draw closer at their table and a bell of intense concentration descended over them. They became extremely active; they lifted their shoulders and eyebrows, kicked their feet, and swayed back

and forth in their chairs. Their in-place motions suggested the twitch-
ings of dreaming dogs. They also looked at one another steadily as
they slipped in and out of various voices, and when they were finished,
the tension dissolved immediately in a barrage of throat-clearings.

Then Biff Burns, a sportscaster (Bob), interviewed Red Finster, of
Astoria (Ray, very chipper), about an upcoming automobile race, in
which Finster, who has no driver's license, will drive a 1958 Edsel. Bob
(stately-voiced) placed a phone call to Harlow W. Barnswell, in King of
Prussia, Pennsylvania. Barnswell (Ray, in a high baritone) turned out
to be the keeper of a lighthouse thirty or forty miles inshore from the
Atlantic. Webley Webster reappeared and began playing the opening
bars of "Jalousie" on the WOR pipe organ. He was interrupted by a
crying baby, whose mother (Ray's falsetto) said there was no stopping
the child once it got going. Artie Schermerhorn (Ray, almost straight-
voiced) did a remote from Port Washington with Professor Selwyn
Hubble (Bob, in his light, husky voice), head of the Hubble Institute of
Penmanship, which teaches aspiring young executives to write illegi-
bly. They came down to Stan Lomax's usual fifteen-minute six-forty-
five sportscast with a discussion of the Bob & Ray Coffeeshop, which
is just along the hall from the studio and whose special that day was a
single boiled potato with parsley for a dollar and nineteen cents. As
Lomax began, Bob and Ray packed up, and they were out of the studio
in a minute flat. They did not say good night to one another. Lomax
finished fifteen seconds before seven o'clock, and Bob and Ray's celebrated signoff, on tape, resounded in the empty studio:

"This is Ray Goulding reminding you to write if you get work,
"And Bob Elliott reminding you to hang by your thumbs."

Fan

JEAN BACH

E. B. White suggests in his essay "Here Is New York" that there are three New Yorks—that of the native-born New Yorker, that of the commuter, and that of "the person who was born somewhere else and came to New York in quest of something." He continues, "Of these three trembling cities the greatest is the last—the city of final destination, the city that is a goal. It is this third city that accounts for New York's high-strung disposition, its poetical deportment, its dedication to the arts, and its incomparable achievements. Commuters give the city its tidal restlessness, natives give it solidity and continuity, but the settlers give it passion." One of the settlers who have given New York immeasurable passion during the past thirty-five years is a pretty, witty, quick, indefatigable woman named Jean Bach. She is a Boswell, for, not widely known herself, she spends much of her time cosseting and studying the great and near-great, the famous and almost famous. She does this in two ways, both of which Boswell would have admired, for each smooths egos and stays vanity. She produces the *Arlene Francis Show*, a radio interview program that has been heard five days a week over WOR for the past twenty-three years, and she gives—often with her husband, Bob Bach—countless select, sought-after parties at her house in Greenwich Village. She picks out the guests for the radio show, reads their books, sees their movies, attends their plays or ballets or art shows, writes the introduction to each interview, and frames questions that Arlene Francis might ask. When a guest fails to appear or Arlene Francis is away, Jean Bach goes on the air, and the show takes on a special sparkle. She talks in a fast, assured Mid-western way, and she has an open, rich voice—the kind that gives the impression of being constantly on the edge of laughter. She has her own patois, made up of a jazz lingo and of her own quick and funny imagery (a good party "flies," a bad one is "a pancake"; a press agent has to "keep all flags flying"; celebrities always "keep their pores open"; her first husband, the late trumpeter Shorty Sherock, was "the first Mr. Bach"). She is also an expert autobiographer. Listeners to the Arlene Francis program know about Jean Bach's feet, which bother her a lot; about her cats, Lena and Lana, who replaced Seymour Katz when he died; about Bob Bach, who is an independent television producer; about her small cinder-block weekend house in the hills of northern Westchester ("It's painted black and green. It looks French. It has angles and corners everywhere that cast pretty shadows"); and about her mother, a beautiful and energetic woman of ninety-one who lives in a Georgian mansion in the middle of Milwaukee. Sometimes people on the show turn up at Jean Bach's parties, and sometimes the people at her parties turn up on the show. She breathes parties and has for most of her life. She also breathes jazz, which she began to listen to when she was a teenager. Her parents gave parties constantly, and she began giving her own when she was fourteen or fifteen. She gave parties for the various sections of the big band that Shorty Sherock had when they were married, and she immediately started giving parties after she and Bob Bach were married, in the late forties. They held charades at their house on Charles Street, and they invited the Herbert Bayard Swopes and the James Downeys and the William Harbachs and the Robert Sarnoffs. The pianist Barbara Carroll provided the first music they had, and she was followed by the likes of Cy Walter and Walter Gross. After Cy Walter played, he would leave a five-dollar bill on the piano— an upright with a short keyboard—as a contribution toward a new piano. They gave a party for Judy Garland. The composer Willard Robison came not because he admired Judy Garland but because he loved the shape of Jean Bach's head, which reminded him of Wendell Willkie's. (Robison drove to the party from White Plains, where he lived, and parked near Jean Bach's house. When he left, he forgot he had driven down and took the train home. Next morning, finding his car missing, he called the police and reported it stolen.) Here are some of the people who have gone to Jean Bach's parties: Geoffrey Holder, Duke Ellington, Billy Strayhorn, Gene Austin, James Mason, Jack Lemmon, Walter Winchell, Vic Damone, Harold Arlen, Yip Harburg, Johnny Mercer, Geraldine Page, Tommy Dorsey, Daphne Hellman, Artie Shaw, James Baldwin, George Wein, Norman Mailer, Burt Bacharach, Rex Reed, Gloria Vanderbilt, Juliette Greco, Randolph Churchill, Sammy Davis, Jr., Mica and Ahmet Ertegun, Nesuhi Ertegun, Lena Horne, Lee and Bob Elliott, and Bobby Short. Short was co-host with Jean Bach of one of the greatest of all Bach parties—a celebration of their forty years of friendship. It was a black-tie dance, and it was given in the winter of 1981 at the Carlyle, and it was presided over by Count Basie's band. The guest list caromed from Tony Bennett to Kurt Vonnegut to Jack Lemmon to Ira Gitler. Jean Bach wore a brilliant full-skirted red dress with a half-moon neck and puffed sleeves, and she looked like an anemone. She has, she has said, been compared with every famous blonde of the twentieth century, among them Doris Day, Shirley Temple, and Ingrid Bergman. She has a handsome nose and blue eyes and a square face.

Bobby Short has said this about his old friend: "Jean and I met in the winter of 1942 at the Sherman Hotel in Chicago. She was married to Shorty Sherock, who was in the Alvino Rey band, and I was singing in the Dome in the hotel. I was a baby just out of high school, and what drew me to Jean was not only her love for Duke Ellington but the fact that she could sing note for note Ben Webster solos and Cootie Williams solos and Johnny Hodges solos. And—she *knew* my idol, Ivie Anderson. Jean was by far the most elegant and beautiful and sharply intelligent person I had ever met. We resumed our friendship in Southern California the following year; then I lost track of her and didn't see her again until Paris in 1952, when our friendship got off on a good adult level. In December of 1981, we celebrated its fortieth anniversary with the dance at the Carlyle. The Basie band's sheer aural power, contained and condensed in those small rooms, was mind-blowing. Jean and I talk at least once a week, and we have never had a quarrel or a disagreement. She never schemes, never makes demands. She's very human, so she's vulnerable, and she's very courageous. She's also loyal and unchanging. She's not one way in Albany one week and another way in New York the next week. And her energy is boundless. She passes information on in the most unassuming manner—it never comes across as a lesson or as an act of self-aggrandizement. She still corrects me, but in the gentlest way. In earlier days, I was sometimes out of work, and I'd always turn to Jean and she'd tell me what to do, and what she told me was invariably right. Our friendship always makes me think how awfully difficult it is to let your friends know in what high esteem you hold them."

Jean Bach's urge to pass information on resulted four years ago in her writing a unique sixty-four-page paperback book called *200 Ways to Conquer "The Blues."* It was sold in supermarkets and it fits in a woman's purse. It sets forth advice on how to fight depression—a condition that 25 percent of the nation is said to be sometimes sunk in. The book is full of folk (and urban) wisdom:

USE THE STAIRS. Whenever possible, use your legs instead of the elevator. It's good for the circulation and, as you develop your vigor, your spirits will rise.

CONCEAL EYESORES. A worn place in the rug doesn't mean much to the casual visitor, but it can become a horror for the person who lives with it and has to see it every time she walks across the room. Think about placing a small scatter rug over it. A folding screen is very useful for hiding all kinds of eyesores. Be imaginative. What about a potted palm?

OPEN A WINDOW. Let some fresh air into the place. A nice breeze feels good and you never know what wonderful, new ideas will blow in on it.

FAKE FEELING GOOD. You may have the most legitimate reason in the world to be unhappy. You may have lost someone important to you, you may have lost your job, you may be a stranger in town, you may be recovering from a broken romance. But when you're with people, don't wear your depression like a badge. You're going to have to learn to fake cheerfulness. Believe it or not, eventually that effort will pay off: you'll actually start feeling happier.

DON'T leave your bed unmade.

Absorbing the information she dispenses is an act Jean Bach loves. She once said, "I was sitting in bed one night doing my homework for the show—reading Peter Prescott's memoir about Choate, as a matter of fact—and suddenly I thought, This is the essence, the best thing in the world, the reason I do what I do: acquiring information."

One spring afternoon in 1983, after a quiet Arlene Francis show, Jean Bach walked from the WOR studios to Lord & Taylor, where she had an appointment to have her nails done. First, she had lunch at the

Café, on the fifth floor. She ordered the sandwich platter and talked about Shorty Sherock, who had died not long before. "He was darling," she said. "He was of Polish and Czech extraction, and he was very handsome. I met him at the Three Deuces in Chicago in 1941, and we were married a few weeks later. He was with Gene Krupa at the time, but he spent every extra moment at the feet of Roy Eldridge, whom he worshipped. When Krupa went out of town for one-nighters, Roy started coming along and sitting in, and the next thing we knew Shorty was out and Roy had been hired. It was simply: Who needs this impostor when we have the real thing right there? Shorty and I had a little apartment we'd paid a month's rent for, and we hocked the golf sticks and my pearls. Then Shorty got a call from Tommy Dorsey, and we joined him in Bluefield, West Virginia. Raymond Scott was next, and, after that, Bob Strong, and Alvino Rey, and, finally, Horace Heidt. By this time, we were living in Malibu in a roomy house, and I was giving parties. Horace Heidt turned the band over to Shorty in 1945, and we got the summer booking at the Glen Island Casino, in New Rochelle. Travel was still very slow and difficult because of the war, so we took only our key men. Shorty and I were jammed into a drawing room with all the band parts, and I'd have nightmares about losing the fourth-trombone book. A big picnic basket Ivie Anderson gave us lasted the whole trip. We rented a house in New Rochelle, and I became band manager. We went on the road in the fall, stopping at places like Selma, Alabama, where I remember hanging clothes to dry on a ceiling fan. We had either kids or old cripples in the band, and when we didn't have enough money to pay everybody I'd ask the kids if they minded being paid next week, and they'd get real concerned and ask me if I had money for breakfast. It was a strange band. We had a soft, floating Basie-type rhythm section and an Italianate trumpet section that played a little sharp and real loud, and it was constant war. By 1948, I'd had enough. I'd had measles on the road, and I was tired. Shorty and I were divorced, and I married Bob Bach. We lived on West Fourth Street at first; then we moved to Charles Street. I got a job at WNEW as a scriptwriter. Radio still had live music, and everything was scripted—the badinage between the announcer and the band-leader, the introductions to recordings. I went on to Edward Bernays, in his public-relations business, and from him to an early television show called *Okay, Mother.* Dennis James was the host, and we had a guest mother every day. People from the audience were asked questions, and if they got them right they won a sewing machine or a Ronson lighter. The show finally sank of its own dreadful weight. I worked for Dick Kollmar's art gallery, and then went with another press agent. One of the clients was a record producer, and part of my job was to go around to radio stations and hand out payola to disk jockeys. I was supposed to figure out on the spot what a particular d.j. was worth—twenty-five, fifty, or a hundred dollars—and hand him the money. I think Dick Clark was the only one who ever refused me. I was with Harry Sobol after that; then I did a year with Rheingold. I started doing the *Arlene Francis Show* in 1960. We broadcast from Sardi's at the beginning, but it got too difficult. One of our early guests was Carl Sandburg, and when Arlene asked him if God was dead he picked up a piece of celery and started eating it, and all you heard over the air while the great man pondered was *crunch, crunch, crunch.*"

After lunch, Jean Bach descended to the beauty salon, and had her nails done. Then she took a Fifth Avenue bus to Eighth Street, and walked a couple of blocks to her house. It was once the studio of Gertrude Vanderbilt Whitney, and it still looks like a studio. The living room is two stories high, and has a huge north window. The room has a fireplace, a grand piano, and assorted pictures (ink drawings by Salvador Dali, a pencil self-portrait by E. E. Cummings), and to one side there is a tiny bedroom and bath known as the Blossom Dearie Suite—so named because the singer had been wont, after practicing on Jean Bach's piano, to stay the night. A stairway leads down to a dining room and kitchen, and another stairway leads up to the master bedroom. Jean Bach was greeted by Lena and Lana. Curtains were drawn over the great window, and the room was cool and dim. Jean Bach made some tea, and then sat down on a sofa, pulled off her shoes, and put her feet on a coffee table.

"I was born in Chicago," she said, "but I grew up on the east side of Milwaukee. I was an only child, and my parents were a Scott Fitzgerald couple. They associated with the well-fixed. They were blue-eyed and good-looking. They rode well. They sang and played the piano. They loved to dance and had a passion for dance bands. When I was ten and eleven, they'd take me with them to hear Ben Bernie and Hal Kemp. They'd invite the bands to dinner or to late-Sunday-morning champagne breakfasts. My father was George Enzinger, Jr., and he'd grown up in St. Louis. His father was a piano teacher and church organist. Daddy remembered a policeman knocking on the screen door and asking 'the professor' if he would teach him to play the 'Maple Leaf Rag.' He did, note by note, and it took six months. Old Mr. Enzinger was plugged into Bach, though, and I remember him whistling Bach fugues up and down the halls. My father was plugged into anything that was avant-garde or anti-establishment. He'd gone to the University of Missouri School of Journalism, and he had his own advertising company. He made monthly trips to New York, where he hung out with the now people of then, like Marion Morehouse, who married E. E. Cummings. She was a fashion model, and Cecil Beaton, or someone like that, said she was one of the two great beauties of the twentieth century. My father would bring back sheet music from the newest shows—songs like Dietz and Schwartz's 'Smokin' Reefers.' And he'd pick up the newest records—Louis Armstrong Hot Fives and Ethel Waters's 'Shake That Thing.' Once, my mother went to California and took the Waters record with her, and when she got back it was broken. My father got very pale and took it into his office and closed the door and spent hours trying to put it together with glue and cardboard. But ordinarily he was a gay, light-hearted man. He'd sit down at the piano at cocktail time and play Chopin, and dinner would be announced and we'd all have to sit and wait, whether the soufflé fell or not. My mother was Gertrude Cole. She was born in Canada, where she lived until she was twelve. Her father was F. F. Cole, the buckwheat king. She was the fourth of six children and the one with all the pizzazz and good looks. When Cole died, the whole troupe moved to Chicago, where they owned land but never seemed to have enough money. Mother taught nursery school at the Hebrew Institute, and she went to the University of Chicago for a while. She had a sister, Viola Cole-Audet, who had trained to be a concert pianist with Harold Bauer. Aunt Viola had a salon in her studio in the Fine Arts Building, and that's where Daddy first met my mother. She thought his name was Anderson, and she told Aunt Viola later that 'that nice Mr. Anderson looked so clean I bet I could have used his toothbrush.' The twenties were a goofy time. There seemed to be nothing but house parties and evening clothes day and night. I remember walking past the music room in our house in Milwaukee on the way to kindergarten and seeing a man in white tie and tails passed out under the piano. There was so much drinking! A German gentleman named Best would go down in our cellar and make liebfraumilch and put it in nice long bottles. So my parents' marriage turned out to be founded on sand. It had no substance. As long as there were parties, they were all right. They were divorced in 1936, and a year later my mother married Eric William Passmore. He was a lawyer and a liberal and a fashion plate, and he eventually became very powerful. He had met Mother when I was one, and had always adored her. In the fifties, he bought her the house she lives in now, and it has Tiffany stair rails and thirteen fireplaces and I don't know how many bathrooms. Eric died in 1979, so I go out on weekends a lot to see her. My father married Irene Castle in 1946. They lived near Chicago, and her friends were famous movie stars. She gave Sunday-evening soirées and posh charity balls, and she'd be invited to the South Side to judge dance contests. Then she and my father moved to Arkansas, where she built a house. He died there in 1959, at the age of sixty-six.

"We moved back to Chicago when I was thirteen, and I went to the University School for Girls. I was class president and editor of the yearbook. I went to Vassar, but I wasn't the drudge I am now, and when my parents were divorced I dropped out and moved into a two-story house with my father in mid-town Chicago. I got a job on the Chicago *Times* as a kind of society columnist for young people—for débutantes, who were very big then. Then I moved over to the Chicago *American*. I was already into jazz, and I'd report on the music they had at the deb parties. Jonah Jones told me a little while ago that I gave him the first mention he ever had in a newspaper. My byline was simply Jean, and I also had a record-review column. I guess I was the first jazz groupie. I'd heard Benny Goodman at the Congress Hotel in 1935 and 1936, and Jimmy Dorsey had taken me to hear Earl Hines at the Grand Terrace. When I was at Vassar, I heard Charlie Barnet at Yale and the old Count Basie band at the University of Virginia. Billie Holiday was singing with him, and I ran into her in the ladies' room. I was gushy, and she wasn't too enchanted. I went out with Roy Eldridge in my late teens. He had a La Salle convertible, and I remember one night he had the guitarist John Collins and the drummer Doc West in the back seat and they'd missed a couple of days of *Terry and the Pirates* and he filled them in on what had happened—but in swing talk: 'This little cat, he had eyes for this chick. But, man, you know, she was called the Dragon Lady, and she was sly . . .' He went on like that, with passion, for half an hour. I also went out with John Bubbles, who had been Sportin' Life in *Porgy and Bess*. Daddy knew Abbie Mitchell, who was in *Porgy*, too, and she introduced us. I visited New York in 1938, and I was backstage at the theatre Bubbles was playing when Stepin Fetchit sent word by one of his footmen that if I wanted his autograph I should stop by where he was working and he'd give it to me and take me on a tour of Harlem. So I went, and what a scene! Stepin Fetchit was slithering around his dressing room in one of the brand-new cashmere suits he'd inherited from the tailor he shared with Rudolph Valentino— who had died before he could wear them. Stepin Fetchit had a piano, and Herman Chittison was sitting at it. Chittison had worked for him early in the thirties, and later Stepin Fetchit had rescued him from some disaster in Egypt. When I arrived, Stepin Fetchit said, 'What do you want to hear? "Tea for Two"? Fine. "Tea for Two," Chittison,' and Chittison played "Tea for Two." Then we toured Harlem in his car and wound up at Jimmy Daniels'.

"In my day, Chicago was very important musically. There was the Club DeLisa and the Grand Terrace and the Regal Theatre, where it was essential to know the stage doorman, Bob Redcross. There was the Three Deuces, where Roy Eldridge and Art Tatum played, and the Congress Hotel and the Pump Room, where John Kirby was, all got up in white tie and tails, and the Panther Room in the Hotel Sherman. Ellington spent a month there in 1940, and I went every night, except the one night when Daddy *made* me stay home. I became the No. 1 Ellington fan. I was in the recording studio the day the band did 'Conga Brava,' and Ellington was already dispensing his jive. They'd do a take, and he'd say, as if it mattered, 'Now, Jean, how's the tempo? Should it be slower or faster?' I'd take him seriously and say, 'Well, maybe it should be slower . . .' I was in the studio when Duke and Jimmy Blanton recorded their famous duets. Ellington had told me, 'Come around. I have a novelty—a bass player who plays in tune.' And there was this kid in a crazy navy-blue pin-striped suit that would knock your eye out. When I first knew Ellington and was a fat eighteen-year-old, I told him that he and Stravinsky were my favorite composers, and he said, 'I'm jealous of Stravinsky.' "

Jean Bach laughed and looked at her watch and said that she had to go to a Fortune Society meeting. She explained that she was on the executive board, that the society had been founded by a press agent named David Rothenberg, and that its purpose was to help rehabilitate former convicts. She said that after the meeting it was early to bed, so that she could get rested for a party she was giving the next night. "It's more or less built around Henry Quarles. He's a lawyer and an Ellington scholar I met recently in Milwaukee when I went to visit my mother. Milwaukee can be very heavy going sometimes. There are a lot of right-wing Republicans and people who like to run down Jews and blacks, and I was going crazy, so I called Henry and he asked me to an Ellington Study Group meeting. They played records and told stories and cheered me up. Later, he wrote and asked me if I was going to their annual meeting in Washington, D.C., and I wrote back and said that I couldn't but that the Blossom Dearie Suite would be vacant and wouldn't he come and stay and I'd give a little party for the group after the Washington meeting. About fifty are coming, including Pat Willard, who's doing an Ellington biography; members from Holland, Belgium, and West Germany; Joya Sherrill, the Ellington singer; Steve James, Duke's nephew; Brooks Kerr; Harold Taylor, who used to be head of Sarah Lawrence and played clarinet at Ellington's seventieth-birthday party at the White House; and such locals as Richard Sudhalter and Dan Morgenstern and Ira Gitler. We'll have ham and macaroni-and-cheese and thin-sliced cucumbers in vinegar. I'm aiming at quantity, because I'm panicked about running out of food. I don't know why, but Ellington fans are heavy eaters." Jean Bach picked up her pocketbook and said: "Someone from out of town I met last night asked me why I live in New York. I told him I live here because of the tempo and the fast track, because there are always so many more choices. I live here because it ruins you for any other place."

WOR cancelled the *Arlene Francis Show* in 1984, and after several rest-less years, Jean Bach, haunted by the famous 1958 Art Kane *Esquire* magazine photograph of fifty-seven jazz musicians standing on a Harlem stoop, decided to try and make a movie about the taking of the photograph. She filmed interviews with all of the dozen or so survivors of the picture, and hired a producer named Matthew Seig and a film editor named Susan Peehl. The movie, just an hour long, was finished in 1994. Called *A Great Day in Harlem*, it is a brilliant, surprising, funny documentary. It was nominated for an Academy Award, has been shown worldwide, and has become both Jean Bach's glory and her payback to the music she has loved so long.

In the Berg

LOLA SZLADITS

Lola Szladits has two profound loves—her husband, Charles Szladits, and the Berg Collection, of which she is curator. Charles Szladits, a professor of law at Columbia, takes care of Lola (as she likes to be called), and Lola takes care of the Berg. Housed in four large rooms on the third floor of the New York Public Library, the Berg is formally known as the Henry W. and Albert A. Berg Collection of English and American Literature, and it contains roughly a hundred and fifty thousand items, among them a letter from Jane Austen to her sister Cassandra, dated November 26, 1815; original drawings by Phiz (Hablot K. Browne) for *"Nicholas Nickleby,"* Emerson's famous printed letter to Walt Whitman praising *"Leaves of Grass,"* and a first edition of that volume; the manuscript of Henry Roth's *"Call It Sleep,"* written in pencil in blue-covered examination books; Fanny Burney's diaries and Virginia Woolf's diaries; a first edition of Daisy Ashford's *"The Young Visitors,"* together with the pencil manuscript, starting "Mr. Salteena was an elderly man of 42 and was fond of asking peaple to stay with him;" a first edition of *"Paradise Lost;"* the manuscript of T. S. Eliot's "The Waste Land," with Ezra Pound's leapfrogging deletions and corrections, the first American edition of the poem (1922), and the Hogarth Press edition (1923), set in type by

Virginia Woolf; "*Two Stories,*" by Virginia Woolf and L. S. Woolf, the first book issued by the Hogarth Press (1917); Jerome Kern's copy of a first edition of "*Alice's Adventures in Wonderland,*" and a dedication copy to Alice Pleasance Liddell, signed by the author; one of the twenty-three known original copies of Blake's "*Songs of Innocence;*" the betrothal copy of Hawthorne's "*Twice-Told Tales,*" signed "Miss Sophia A. Peabody, with the affectionate regards of her friend, Nath. Hawthorne;" the man-uscript of Winston Churchill's obituary of Rupert Brooke, done for the London *Times*; Carl Van Vechten's (No. 366) and James Stephens's (No. 474) copies of the first edition of Joyce's "*Ulysses*" (a thousand copies were printed); Wilkie Collins's edition of Dickens's collected works; Charlotte Brontë's travelling desk; and the papers of Lady Gregory and of May Sarton. The Berg Collection was begun in 1906 by two promi-nent New York physicians, Henry W. Berg and Albert A. Berg. The eld-est and the youngest of eight children of a poor Hungarian who came to the United States in 1862, Henry and Albert eventually lived as bachelors in a town house on Seventy-third Street, just off Fifth Avenue. They practiced at Mt. Sinai. Henry Berg died in 1938, and a little over a year later Albert presented to the New York Public Library thirty-five hundred items the brothers had collected. Not long after, he bought and added sixteen thousand pieces (the W. T. H. Howe collection) and then fifteen thousand pieces (the Owen D. Young collection). John D. Gordan, a former Harvard English instructor and a Conrad expert, was appointed the first curator of the Berg, in 1940, and he continued to add to the collection until his death, in 1968. (Albert Berg died in 1950.) Lola Szladits was appointed curator in 1969, and, in turn, has continued to add to the collection. Her most famous acquisition is probably the Auden papers, some of which came to the Berg only after an arduous legal battle.

Qualified researchers (generally no college undergraduates) use the collection in the great oak study room, which is lined on two walls with hundreds of hand-tooled leather slipcases filled with Thackeray and Dickens. The public gets glimpses of the Berg at its semiannual exhibitions, mounted next door, in an even larger exhibition room. One of the best of these shows was called "1922: A Vintage Year," and it included a hundred and seventy-five things written or published in America and England during that miraculous year. Among them are "The Waste Land," "*Ulysses,*" Fitzgerald's "*The Beautiful and Damned,*" Galsworthy's *Forsyte Saga,* Katherine Mansfield's *The Garden Party and Other Stories,* Booth Tarkington's *Gentle Julia,* James Weldon Johnson's *The Book of American Negro Poetry,* D. H. Lawrence's *Aaron's Rod,* E. E. Cummings' *The Enormous Room,* Edna St. Vincent Millay's *The Ballad of the Harp-Weaver,* Sinclair Lewis's *Babbitt,* Willa Cather's *One of Ours,* A. E. Housman's *Last Poems,* Virginia Woolf's *Jacob's Room,* John Peale Bishop and Edmund Wilson's *The Undertaker's Garland,* Yeats's *Later Poems,* and the first English translation of Proust's *Swann's Way.* Handsome catalogues accompany these exhibits, and from time to time the Berg publishes books. Generally, they are facsimile editions of holdings, and a recent one is of Dickens's *Memoranda* book, kept in 1855 and containing ideas and descriptions he had jotted down, along with lists of possible names for characters. Fred Kaplan, who edited the facsimile, points out that many of the names may have come from the parish register of St. Andrew's Church, Holborn. (So much for Dickens's long-celebrated genius for inventing onomatopoeic names!) From these lists, Twemlow turns up in *Our Mutual Friend,* Magwitch in *Great Expectations,* Stiltstalking in *Little Dorrit* (Dorrit is a variation of Dorret, which also appears at St. Andrew's), and Carton in *A Tale of Two Cities.* These names were never used: Snosswell, Squab, Pordage, Pemble, Jee, and Spessifer.

Lola Szladits talks about the Berg with passion: "We protect the written word at the Berg. It is a research collection, not a museum. It has to be used. It is alive. My role at the Berg is to stand still and allow the collection to grow. In fact, I try to make time itself stand still here. I try to create quiet and the timelessness that allows for the pursuit of truth. The young, especially, need a great deal of time. I might buy well or badly for the collection—that is intellectual judgment. But I would reap havoc or madness by confusing our users—by not sizing up a question from a caller or correspondent and sending him in the proper direction or helping him discover it himself. I have been fortunate in having the right advisers at the right time. John Gordan, who brought me into the Berg, in 1955, marked me for life. When he was here, we were very gay. He would roar like a lion in his magnificent baritone or sing like a bird. He used to sing all of *Pal Joey*. We laughed so hard sometimes people heard us through our closed doors. But he had another side. He was a misogynist, who used to tell me only men had a chance for promotion here. And he had a terrible temper—even though it only lasted five minutes. I grew up very fast during my first year or two as curator.

"There are first-rate collections all over the United States now, but no collection has everything. My great pride in the Berg is that everything fits. The Huntington Library, in San Marino, California, is a paradise, and it has a beautiful illuminated manuscript of *The Canterbury Tales*. The Houghton Library, at Harvard, has Keats and the Samuel Johnson collection put together by the American collectors of eighteenth-century literature Donald and Mary Hyde. Yale has the Boswell papers and Horace Walpole's letters, collected by Wilmarth Lewis. It also has Gertrude Stein. There is an extraordinary collection at the University of Virginia. It has Faulkner manuscripts. The Morgan Library has Thoreau's journal, and it has Hawthorne. The Princeton Library has Fitzgerald and Maxwell Perkins. Between 1956 and 1970, the University of Texas was probably the biggest of all university collectors. It had oil money and could buy anything. It got Evelyn Waugh, the Alfred Knopf collection, Ford Madox Ford, the largest Shaw collection. The English and American collection at the University of Tulsa is beginning to shine. It bought Edmund Wilson's library. And one must never forget the Library of Congress, and the Folger Shakespeare Library, and the Joseph Regenstein Library at the University of Chicago—and the rare-books division of the New York Public Library, which is terribly important and far larger than we are."

Lola Szladits takes care of the Berg five days a week. (It is shut Thursdays and Sundays.) Her office is a long, rectangular room that shoots off at a right angle from the northeast corner of the study room. One wall is lined with shelves holding materials waiting to be catalogued. At the rear of the room, Lola has her desk, and close by are her assistant, Brian McInerney, and her cataloguer, Patrick Lawlor. They are her amanuenses, helpmeets, slaves. Once or twice an hour, peremptory commands issue from Lola's desk—"Brian, please. Find me Emerson's letter to Whitman." "Patrick, please. I would like Tenniel's drawings for *Alice*." "Brian, please. Bring me the manuscript of Yeats's 'Wild Swans at Coole' "—and Brian or Patrick disappears into the stack area, a big two-story temperature-controlled room adjacent to the office. Lola is short and dresses snappily. She wears her gray hair in a closely controlled version of what used to be called a feather cut. She has egg cheeks and sharp, deep-brown eyes. She talks quickly and explosively, with a slight Middle-European accent, and she has a steep, sudden laugh. One quiet day, when few research calls came in, when Patrick was away and Brian was at work on the papers of Jean Garrigue, when the study room was empty and the exhibition room had only a handful of lookers-in, Lola sat at her desk and talked of her life and work. The occasional passages that are in parentheses have been taken from her unpublished autobiography, "Journey of a Heart." Her two voices—speaking and written—are surprisingly close.

"I was born Lola Leontin Abel, in Budapest, in 1923," she said. "What I saw from 1923 to 1929 was happiness and the most privileged view that any child could have. (Time was available, always, everyone seemed to have endless amounts of time in our society and in the twenties: time on street corners, time in coffeehouses, time around dinner tables, time to take long walks, long rides, time to spin out conversation.) I lived in a beautiful apartment in a beautiful house on a beautiful street of a beautiful city. I had a brother, Egon, who was two years older. (He was physically weaker than I, was less resistant, more withdrawn, and much gentler.) I was robust, outgoing, cheerful, impatient—a very sunny child. I was spoiled but disciplined. My brother was extremely watchful, skeptical. He was the most brilliant young man I have ever known. He had strange posture, with his head to one side. I was surrounded by a German governess, a household of servants, innumerable aunts and uncles, a maternal grandfather and grandmother, and a paternal grandmother. (Since my brother and I were new toys to play with in a large family, aunts and uncles came in an endless stream. Some would settle into our little chairs, eat from our little plates, vigorously protesting that they only wished to have a taste. Some would sit at the bedside and tell stories, some leaned against the beautiful handmade tiles covering the ovens to warm their hands. They all clasped their hands behind their backs. Most hands caressed, but the uncles had strong grips. The whiskered uncles kissed, and I developed rashes.) The house we grew up in had been built by my mother's father in 1892 on the site of his father's drygoods store. It was a four-story Gothic building, modelled on a Venetian palace. (Grandfather commissioned one of Hungary's leading painters, Kàroly Lotz, to decorate the façade of his house with two figures—one representing music, the other dance. Artists also covered the gray vaults of the balconies. An azure-blue sky studded with silver stars looked down on me when in balmy weather I stretched out under them or waited for the lamplighter, who, in the twenties, still climbed a ladder to turn on the gaslight.) We had a salon in the Moorish gilt style, with an extraordinary red-glass chandelier. The dining room had Gothic wood-work, and was forty-five feet long. It had stained-glass windows and huge carved Gothic chairs, with green velvet upholstery and bolsters that hit you in the back of the neck. The paintings in the house included a *Passion of Christ* by a member of the Munich School, and one called *The Dream*, in which a reclining lady was being served coffee by a monkey. When my mother and father were married, in 1919, she was twenty-six and he was thirty-nine. My grandfather gave them an apartment in the house, and after I was born my grandparents moved into a villa even more luxurious than our house. We visited them every Sunday and stayed all day. My mother's twin brother, who had an unhappy life, and her older sister and younger brother, who was my grandparents' pet, also lived there, in their own apartments. My grandfather was born in 1860, and he was small and fast-moving. He was crazy about aviation, and he had a picture of himself standing near a zeppelin. In 1927, there was no peace about Lindbergh. We ate it noon and night. And my grandfather's house was full of radios. His love of his first house was contagious, and it became the house where I walked in later years in my dreams. His love was so strong that in the early forties he shipped a piece of Carrara marble to Budapest and had it carved in the shape of the doorway to the house and placed it in the cemetery as his tombstone. He also had a plaster model of the tombstone on his desk. My grandmother was patient and lovely. She spoke Hungarian with a Slovak accent. My first language was Hungarian, but there were Italian noises in the house, and some Serbian. (Even in my close family, there were those who were less well off than we were. Every Saturday afternoon, we visited Father's mother, who lived on a widow's pension. . . . I don't believe I ever saw my father embrace his mother, and during those twenty years I knew her she remained no more than a presence to me. The joy of visiting her was supplied by the coachman who allowed me to hold the reins, and by a canary Grandmother Rosa kept. . . . At Grandmother Rosa's, it was always very cold, and she always sat in a rocker wrapped in shawls. She lived in a small apartment, which had only one portrait—that of my grandfather whom I never knew, who had been a mechanical engineer on the National Railroad. . . . Apart from my uncles, a widowed aunt shared Grandmother Rosa's house; after her husband's death she cried most of the time.) My father's older brother had travelled in Turkey and America, and he was a mechanical engineer. He had seen the George Washington Bridge and, being from Budapest, a city of bridges, he loved to talk about it. I never heard my father's younger brother say a single word. I remember Grandmother Rosa's hands—she was always knitting.

"When my brother was born, my parents bought a summer cottage on Lake Balaton. It was three hours by train from Budapest, and we spent the summer there. Everything was made by peasants. The dining room was blue, with floral painting and peasant carving. Cornfields stretched for miles, and the meadows were full of sheep. We had a well, and our water was stored in a cistern in the attic. There was no electricity. There was a rose garden and an orchard and a barnyard, all tended by a gardener who lived there year round.

"My mother was not attractive. She was only four feet eight. But she was quite astonishing. She was emancipated. She read in German, French, Hungarian, and English. She read history. She was into the avant-garde of Hungarian literature. She did all this very quietly, very subtly. She never showed off. My father was a simple man, almost transparent. He was quiet, gentle, and sweet. He was not a social being. Much of the time he did what my mother told him to do—without murmuring. When the Depression came, my father lost his job. He had been a 'Mr. Director' in the Teudloff-Dietrich factory, but it went bankrupt and was dismantled by its creditors. He could not find work. He heard that the Americans had discovered oil near the Austro-Hungarian border, and with my mother pushing him he ended up a 'Mr. Director' with a subsidiary of Standard Oil of New Jersey."

Brian went out for lunch, and Lola made a phone call. Then she looked into the study room and the exhibition room. The study room had one visitor in it, and the exhibition room had a dozen or so. When Brian returned, Lola descended four flights to the library cafeteria, which is in the basement near the loading area. She had a tuna-fish-salad sandwich and coffee. After lunch, she visited the gleamingly revamped Periodical Room, on the main floor, and ascended by elevator to the Berg. She said hello about twenty times during her trip.

"When I started at the Lutheran Elementary School, I already knew how to read and write," Lola said. "Our German governess left in 1930, and a nineteen-year-old English girl, Marjorie Wolff, came for the summer and stayed until 1941, when she took the last train back to England. She had come from a convent, and she grew into a ravishing young lady. She left many battered hearts behind. She taught us English with charades and very little discipline. She was a real pal to me, and she shaped my mind to a degree that only I know. After elementary school, I went to a sort of progressive *Gymnasium*, from which I graduated in 1941. I never received a grade below A in any subject. My brother and I went to the University of Budapest. He was at the law school, and I took English and French literature, with a minor in art history. (I visited many of my friends whose families owned land; continued to play a good game of tennis; held my grandfather's weakening elbow on the skating rink; and turned into one of those strange twenty-year-old girls who are confided in and have no confidences to share.) Hitler had marched into Vienna in 1938, and the Germans arrived in Budapest on March 19, 1944. On April 2, my father's two brothers and his widowed sister killed themselves. Grandmother Rosa had already died, aged ninety. My brother became an auxiliary Army worker, and I took a job in a French cotton factory and lived in a dormitory in the factory. My father resigned from the oil company. My grandparents were driven from their villa and ended in an old people's home. I became a wild thing. I met a French Army deserter in the factory and spent a couple of platonic nights in his mistress's attic, quite far from the city. I remember he said, 'What is the use of having you here? You don't know how to cook or make love.' I recited French poets to him at night, and during the day we travelled the trams, passing unnoticed among Germans and Hungarian Nazis. I stayed with a Swiss friend of my father's, and I stayed with a friend who had a room at a policeman's house. When the Russians besieged Budapest, late in 1944, my mother and father and I were living in a cellar on the edge of a park, my father out scavenging for food and me cooking weak stews. The last time I saw my brother, I begged him to get out, to escape, but he didn't have the courage. I still have my guilt: I should have made him leave. He died somewhere in the west of Hungary, either shot or from typhoid. The siege lasted fifty days, and Budapest was indescribable when it was over—the beautiful bridges gone, the streets full of dead, a terrible stink everywhere. We moved back into our house, which had not been badly wrecked, and I took what furniture I could out of my grandfather's villa, which had been desecrated. I brought it by degrees in a small pushcart to our house—I do not to this day know how. I had already decided I would have nothing to do with rebuilding Budapest. I had decided I would go to America.

"The American Military Mission arrived in April of 1945, and I got a job as a secretary and a translator. I worked for Colonel Richard Shackelford, who introduced penicillin into Hungary and became our saint. I occasionally took trips around the country with him, translating for him. I took some time off and did my thesis. It was a comparative study of the psychological effects of children's literature on English and Middle-European children. I took my degree summa cum laude. That was early in 1946, and it was then that I wrote to Columbia University asking for a scholarship. I had heard through the American cultural officer, Tom Riegel, that there were frozen Hungarian funds over here that might be accessible. He wrote to Columbia, too. Columbia finally said yes, and that I could start late that year. I got a passport, a student visa, and clearance from the Russians, who had taken over my beloved country. I raised two thousand dollars in American bills to take with me. I tried to tell my parents what Russia would do to our country, and was told, 'What does a twenty-three-year-old know of politics?' They were appalled that I was leaving, and when Grandfather heard he said he would disinherit me—although he had no idea he no longer had anything to disinherit anyone with. I flew in an American plane to London, where Marjorie Wolff met me, and by November I was in New York.

"A year later, I was on the *Queen Mary* with my mother on my way back to London. I had exhilarating beginnings in America—travelling to Washington and Chicago, making friends easily, enjoying the wide-openness of New York just after the war. I got engaged and broke the engagement. I worked too hard and didn't get enough sleep. I did crazy things. I was very depressed. I had written my mother three times a week, and by the fall of 1947 she got the signal something was wrong. In England, I recovered. My mother left me in London and went back to Budapest. I met Charles Szladits, whom I had known slightly in Budapest, and who was to become my husband in 1950. I got a job as a medical librarian at Oxford but was fired after six weeks for talking indiscreetly about politics. In 1948, I enrolled in library school in London, and supported myself by typing and by giving English lessons to an aging Hungarian couple. Sometimes I was hungry. Then what I feared would happen happened. My father was arrested. The Communists had taken over all foreign and privately owned companies, Standard Oil among them. He was tried on bogus charges and was sentenced to ten years. He was in his late sixties. He spent five years in prison, and died in September of 1953, whether by murder or from starving to death we shall never know. Charles and I had come to America in 1950. In 1955, my mother managed to get a passport and went to London, finally arriving in New York in 1956. She took over our household, then moved into her own apartment in Butler Hall. She was sixty-four, and insisted that she work. She sewed pearls on sweaters—pearls were the rage—and finally she became a medical-records librarian at Columbus Hospital. She loved New York, and went to all the free concerts and sat in the Family Circle at the opera. She died of leukemia in January of 1960. She had not told anyone about it. I don't think she even told herself.

"Between the time I came back to New York with Charles and November of 1955, when I was hired as an assistant at the Berg, I worked for a Park Avenue advertising agency, in the periodicals room and rare-book division of the beautiful Academy of Medicine, and as an art librarian at the New York Public Library. That was not a happy job for me. Brian, please. Get me my 'Statement of Professional Achievement,' which I did two years ago." When Brian returned with it, Lola read this aloud: "In the Art Division of the New York Public Library I served with no distinction from March to November, 1955. I expected a different, more specialized public from the one we had, and the professional work assigned to me was too clerical for my highbrow aspirations. I was at the reference desk for two hours; answered reference letters which required 'at most one hour;' sorted a vast clipping file and clipped daily art items from the *Times*. The staff had avant-garde tastes and my 'classical profile' isolated me from my peers, who perceived someone very different from them. The service review I received— the first one I had ever seen—was very bad indeed: I discriminated among the readers (I had spent a couple of hours with Aldous Huxley, ignoring everyone else); the questions that interested me received too close attention; telephone questions had been answered without my referring to 'at least two reference books;' I got along badly with the staff. Much of what was objectionable, wrote my supervisor, could in time be eliminated, because the clue was in my personality. I did not see how that could be changed, but I did by then hear of a vacancy that arose in the Berg Collection."

The phone rang, and Lola talked for several minutes. She said after she hung up that a scholar named Bart Winer had just told her he had heard that the Nabokov papers were available. Lola said there was nothing she wanted more for the Berg, and she fired off a telegram to Véra Nabokov in Montreux: "B. WINER TELLS ME YOU WISH TO SELL ARCHIVE. LETTER FOLLOWS FROM THE BERG COLLECTION, THE NEW YORK PUBLIC LIBRARY. CORDIALLY, NABOKOV'S GREAT ADMIRER AND YOUR FRIEND, LOLA SZLADITS, CURATOR, BERG COLLECTION."

"Love of literature has little to do with this sort of thing," Lola said. "This is pure business. You have no idea how many hard-hitting literary widows there are in the world. So, anyway, you see what I was like until John Gordan took me over, until New York took me over. New York has become my natural habitat. I'd be fenced in anywhere else.

I can behave exactly as I want: I can appear, I can disappear. It's lovely to see Park Avenue dressed in green in the summer and to see the roses in front of the library. It's lovely to walk near the Hudson and down tree-filled side streets. I love the early-morning light. The morning crowd is a little like a small town—people say good morning. When I'm in Europe on book-buying trips, I miss New York, and sometimes Europe doesn't compare well. London slows you down. Rome is too crowded. Munich is a showcase. Zurich hems you in.

"Charles's and my marriage works because we leave each other alone. He's a remarkable man. He was born in Budapest, in 1911. His father was a professor of law and a judge, and his mother was very strong. They were marvellous parents, and supported Charles and his older brother in everything they did. Charles went to law school in Budapest and started out in the Ministry of Justice. He took another law degree at the London School of Economics after the war, and studied at Columbia, where he still is—at the Parker School of Foreign and Comparative Law. Charles's great work is his bibliography of foreign and comparative law, seven or eight volumes of which have been published since 1955. It is known in law simply as 'the Szladits.' Charles is very routine-minded. In the morning, I read the paper in bed, and Charles prepares my breakfast—orange juice, coffee, a fruit salad with five or six different kinds of fruit. Then he exercises, doing twenty-five pushups. He runs around the living room while listening to the news on the radio. I talk all the time, slowly get ready, and leave for work. He sees me to the door. Charles reads the *Times* and has his breakfast. I call him when I get to work and, soon after, he goes to work. At one sharp, he has lunch with Nina Galston—Mrs. Clarence Galston—who is the editor of a series of legal publications put out by the Parker School. They have had lunch together for thirty-four years. After lunch, Charles walks home. (We live near Columbia.) He looks at the mail, brews his coffee, and has some fresh fruit. Then he has a short nap, and goes back to work. I try to be home to hear the six o'clock news on WQXR. When Charles returns, I am lying down and talking, and after he listens a while he excuses himself and says, 'I have to bread the chicken,' or 'I have to see to the spinach.' He is a good, reliable cook. I join him in the kitchen, and we eat and talk until eight-thirty. I fall asleep early. When we go out, it's to the Philharmonic or to the movies or to book affairs. If he doesn't want to go to the book things, he stays home. We dine out in the neighborhood. On Saturday, I leave the library at midday. By the time I get home, Charles has done the vacuuming, and he has already been to Zabar's. We watch my diet. We have lunch and I have a nap—two hours. Saturday night, he buys the early edition of the Sunday *Times*. We have a late breakfast on Sundays. Sometimes we take a walk on Riverside Drive or Broadway. Sometimes we go to the Metropolitan Museum or the National Academy of Design. We used to spend weekends at Mohonk or visit friends in the suburbs, but we don't seem to do that much anymore. We never exchange harsh words. If I get impatient, I shut up. It took a long time to know Charles. He is very reserved. A one-to-one person. A silent person. He spoils me."

Harp Lady

DAPHNE HELLMAN

Wherever she goes, Daphne camps out. She even slips in and out of her names. She was born Daphne Bayne but became Daphne Bull. After that, she was Daphne Hellman, then Daphne Shih. Now she is known by her friends and colleagues simply as Daphne. They all know who they are talking about when they run into one another and say "How's Daphne?" or "Daphne has a bad cold" or "Daphne just left for Australia." She is a woman of means, who owns three houses—one in the East Sixties; one on a hilltop in St. James, Long Island; and one on another hilltop, in Truro, on Cape Cod—but she never stays in any of them long. She may light in Manhattan for four or five days, then drive out to St. James, but only for a night or two. (Her adopted son, Digger St. John, lives there.) Or she'll run down South for a series of one-nighters with her trio, Hellman's Angels (Daphne on harp, Eddie Berg on guitar, Lyn Christie on bass). Or she'll do Russia or India or Australia or Sri Lanka with the trio. Or she'll look in on her son Benjy Bull, a greatly talented guitarist, who lives in Brentwood, California. Or she'll run over to Paris for a couple of weeks and play her harp on the street with the violinist Colette Lepage and the bassist Jack Gregg. (Daphne's daughter, Daisy Paradis, a gifted sitar player, is living there now, too.)

Or she'll go on an Earthwatch expedition to Kenya or Madagascar or China or Panama. But there are three absolutes in her life: New York (through her Bayne Fund she contributes to the Metropolitan Museum, the American Museum of Natural History, the Bronx Zoo, and the Museum of the City of New York); the harp; and the Village Gate, where she has appeared every Tuesday (when she is in town) for twenty-eight years. (It may be the longest-running night-club gig in the history of New York.)

On a recent Tuesday morning, not long after she had taken her daily outing on roller skates, Daphne talked about harps and harpists in her New York living room: "Everyone knows what a harp looks like, but not many people know how difficult it is to play. There are six or seven octaves on the average concert harp, and each octave has seven strings. The strings are colored: the C's are red, the F's blue, and so on. Without this, it would be hard to tell where you are. You pluck the strings with your thumbs and with the first three fingers of each hand—the pinkies are too short and weak. The strings are regulated by seven pedals, placed in a semicircle at the base of the post and attached to rods inside the post, which are hooked to the strings by little pins. One pedal controls the C strings, one the D's, and so forth. Each pedal can be depressed two notches, and each notch shortens the string a half-tone. The harp is tuned in C-flat, so if you depress the C pedal one notch you get a C, and two notches gives you a C-sharp. That is the great difficulty of harp playing: you have to think with your feet.

"There are eight thousand harpists in this country and they make a cozy, intense world. Harpists work in symphony orchestras and in the studios and in hotels and leisure places. A good gold concert harp can cost twenty thousand dollars. I'm lucky enough to be able to buy harps, and I keep one here, one in St. James, and one in Truro. There's another at the Metropolis Café, on Union Square, where I play Sunday lunches, one at the Gate, and one at Kitty O'Shea's little restaurant near my house. I also have a travelling harp in my van. And I've rented one out to the 'Fantasticks' company for years, at eighty dollars a month."

Daphne's living room is nearly two stories high and has floor-to-ceiling windows on the south which look into a garden. A gold harp, an upright piano, an electric keyboard, and a Gravikord were gathered against the west side of the room. (The Gravikord is a stringed instrument shaped like a fishing rod which was invented by her friend the trombonist Bob Grawi. She uses it when she plays in the subway.) On the walls were a William Burroughs abstraction, a Warren Miller cartoon of a big band made up of eighteen accordionists and a drummer, an early Paul Resika oil of a Cape Cod beach, a Saul Steinberg interior, an Al Hirschfeld drawing of Daphne at her harp, and, in a corner, a small Robert White terra-cotta sculpture of Digger St. John. Daphne does not believe in spending money on furniture, and the various pieces in the room looked exhausted. She loves birds, and on an end table next to her was a big birdcage containing an African glossy starling. She said that she bought the bird thirteen years ago, and that it not only sings, it barks. She also said that she had owned an English blackbird that sang at four-thirty every morning in the spring. At one time, she had so many large birds in the living room and adjacent kitchen that they tended to outshout the humans, causing her old friend Rogers Whitaker to describe the place as "helter-skelter palace." Daphne herself is birdlike. She has a narrow, handsome face and short blond hair. Although she probably weighs under a hundred pounds, she is still shapely, and has a firm grip and a viola voice. She loves to laugh, and she talks with the explosive frankness of someone who has taken long inward looks and found what she saw acceptable.

"My mother was responsible for getting me started on the harp," she continued. "I was born in New York, in 1915, right in my parents' apartment, at 820 Park. I had a sister, Betty, who was four years older. When I was seven and she was eleven, our parents moved us to Morristown, New Jersey, so that we wouldn't get any more colds, but, of course, we got everything. My father's name was Howard Bayne. He was one of five children, and he was born in Ireland. His father, Samuel Bayne, had a house on Riverside Drive, and he had a parrot that bit us and laughed when we cried. My father's sister Emily married an English architect and member of Parliament, Lord Alfred Bossom. When Winston Churchill first heard the name, he asked how to spell it, and said, 'Well, it's neither one nor the other, is it?' My father was handsome and short and straight-featured. He had a flashing smile and blue-green eyes. He liked to drink, and when he did he became conversational. When he was in his late sixties, he was told to stop drinking and smoking, but it didn't work for him. He had wanted to be an electrical engineer, but his father made him go into banking, and he did. My grandfather had a hand in founding the Chase Manhattan Bank, and he had also worked in the oil fields and published a book about it, called *Derricks of Destiny*. My mother was Louise Van Beuren, and she was born at 21 West Fourteenth Street. One of her brothers was a surgeon at Presbyterian Hospital, and another cut a swath in Newport. My mother had mucho money. I adored her when I was little. She was not pretty, but she was tall and vivacious and had expressive eyebrows. She talked a great deal. My sister and I were very close, but we each had our own governess, and they were rather mean to us. Mine made me take long, lonely walks, and she didn't like me to see my friends. But of course we learned to speak French. When I was around nine, Mother started to be critical of everything—whether we were clean, how we dressed, our manners. I took refuge in animals. I began collecting bats, which I'd find behind shutters. I still love them. They are much maligned and misunderstood. And I sent away for armadillos."

When she was ten, Daphne kept a diary, and she still has it. It has a nice Daisy Ashford ring. Here is her first meeting with a bat (the entry is dated Friday, April 3, 1925: the place is Morristown): "One morning I woke up and went to see my pets, and looking in my basin of fish I saw two dark objects trying to get out. I took them and put them on my pillow and peted and kissed them but one bit me. I looked closly and saw that my visitors had wings and very big ears, a darling but very wicked face, sharp white teeth, sharp claws and soft brown fur. Now that they were dry I saw that they were bats. Evidently they had flown in the window and trying to get a drink, fell in for bats need much water. Then they flew around the room and we put blankets around our heads for fear they should get in our hair. They got behind the screens and scrached themselves then hiched on to the heater and made faces at us. That afternoon I caught them and let them go. They looked like spiders when they were on the floor."

Leaning forward, Daphne continued, "I went first to the Peck School, in Morristown, then to Ethel Walker's for a year. I whined that it was too strict, so I was put in Farmington, which I really liked. From there I went to Chapin, in New York, and in the winter of 1933–34 I came out. I decided I wanted to try acting, and I enrolled in the American Academy of Dramatic Arts, and after that I went to the Royal Academy in London for a year. I had a walk-on part in Leslie Howard's *Hamlet*, in New York, which didn't get very good reviews. Then I met my first husband, Harry Bull. He was the editor of *Town & Country*, and he was eleven years older than I was. My family didn't think much of Harry, but I married him anyway. I was twenty-one. He was a strange man, very sarcastic, but I was an awful wife. Unfaithful. I modelled for *Harper's Bazaar* and for *Town & Country*. I modelled for Man Ray. Jerome Zerbe photographed me. I was a cover girl. I started to dye my hair blond and tried to look like Veronica Lake.

"I had a stillborn child in 1939, because I was Rh-negative; then Benjy Bull was born. In 1940, I fell in love with Geoffrey Hellman, a *New Yorker* writer. He was a tall lighthouse of a fellow whose only sin was eating. When Benjy was two, Harry Bull, who had detectives watching Geoffrey and me, quit *Town & Country*, kidnapped Benjy, and moved to Florida. Benjy didn't live with me again until he was ten. Geoffrey and I were married in Reno in 1941, and his mother came on our honeymoon. My sister married three money men, and I married three literary men. Geoffrey was in the O.S.S. during the war, and we lived in Washington, D.C., and got to know people like Eddie Newhouse and Saul Steinberg and Robert Lewis Taylor. I had taken classical harp lessons with Mildred Dilling for years, but had given up the harp in my teens; the Spanish harpist Nicanor Zabaleta had a great deal to do with getting me back to it. When we returned to New York after the war, I played in a concert at Town Hall with the diseuse Marianne Oswald. *Time* said I was 'as curvesome as a treble clef.' I began getting a lot of work as a harpist. In the fifties I started studying jazz harp with Phyllis Pinkerton, who had been taught by Lennie Tristano. She made me sing intervals and clap two against three and practice with a metronome. She made me sing along with Lester Young records, then sing the solos without the records. And she made me play along with his solos, then play them by myself.

"I played with Ving Merlin and his All-Girl Band at the Hotel New Yorker, and I was at Billy Rose's Diamond Horseshoe. Then I came under Julius Monk's jovial management, and worked at the Upstairs at the Downstairs with Julius and Stella Brooks and Imogene Coca and Blossom Dearie and Annie Ross. And I worked at the Ruban Bleu and the Versailles and Le Perroquet. Summers, we all went to the Atlantic House in Provincetown. Norman Mailer was there, and Tennessee Williams, and Hugh Shannon. Daisy Hellman was born to Geoffrey and me in 1946, and in 1951 I adopted Digger St. John. He was a three-year-old Irish baby, and I found him largely through John McCarten's sister, who lived in Ireland. Geoffrey had a lot of lady friends and I had men friends, and we made the mistake of telling each other what we were doing. Geoffrey decided, finally, that he wanted a divorce, and he remarried. In 1961, I married Hsio-Wen Shih, a brilliant architect and writer, but one day in 1965 he just disappeared. I was devastated. People have told me that they have seen him in England, but I have never heard a word from him since, and he has never touched a penny of the trust fund I set up for him. I have had a lot of beaux since then—an art dealer, a psychiatrist, a writer—but I'm still married to Wen."

People love to talk about Daphne. Here are three voices. The first belongs to Marty Hall, a painter who divides her time between a tiny apartment in the East Eighties and a house she shares in Wellfleet with her husband, Jack, who is also a painter. "I like Daphne because she's an original, and she has this enormous energy," she said the other day. "I like it that she has played the harp so eclectically. She's a total performer. She's headstrong, and she does what she wants. Jack remembers her from dancing-school days in New York. She was very beautiful and very shy. Up until about ten years ago, this shyness made it difficult to carry on a relaxed conversation with her, particularly on the telephone. But in groups she has always had great social poise. I think she must be deeply lonely, or she wouldn't run so."

The second voice is that of Julius Monk: "I think I gave Daphne her first professional job. It was at the Ruban Bleu when it was in the Hotel Langdon, at Fifty-sixth and Fifth. The war was still on, and Geoffrey was in Washington. She took a tiny suite in the hotel, and on opening night there was this blond goddess, this tableau on that tiny stage. After the war, we played at the Bœuf sur la Toit in Paris. We did

Jerome Kern, and to keep her out of trouble we glissed a great deal. Daphne worked the Ruban Bleu twice a year, and once when she was there we hired Billie Holiday. I believe it was Billie's East Side début, and we had a terrible time with her opening night, because she was zonked and refused to share our only dressing room with Daphne. She said, 'I'm not going in that dressing room with that East Side lady'—only she didn't use the word 'lady.' Daphne accepts conditions and people and backgrounds as they are. She faces things and is astonishingly brave. I've seen her do any number of kind things for any number of people. I think at times she has been musically unfulfilled, but she is always questing."

Saul Steinberg issues his extraordinary visions from his studio in Springs, Long Island. He is an acute observer, and his Romanian English makes whatever he says sound like law. "I met Daphne in 1942 or 1943," he said. "I had my first show in America at Betty Parsons' gallery in New York, and she and Geoffrey came and bought two pictures. That was a big thing, you know. In one of the pictures I made a satire of a *National Geographic* magazine cover—a geographer looking at nudity, which was a big feature of the *Geographic* at that time. I was stationed in Washington briefly in 1945, and I saw her and Geoffrey there. I started going to her parties when she bought her house on the East Side. The living room was very formal and elegant then, and had a winding staircase going down to a big dining room. These parties, sui generis, became a kind of salon. There were writers and musicians and artists and publishers. Geoffrey began to behave like the husband of a woman who keeps a salon. He had the attitude of someone visiting a kindergarten. Then he would retire upstairs to bed. I admired Daphne because she reminded me of one of those hillbilly jeep drivers in the service—skinny, tough, and driving like a cowboy."

The African starling barked, and Daphne told it to be quiet. The bird must have reminded her of Africa and Earthwatch. "Tee Addams,

Charlie Addams's widow, took me on my first Earthwatch expedition, in 1980," she said. "Earthwatch was started in 1971. It asks interested people like me to go on scientific expeditions as paying volunteers and worker-observers. The purpose of our trip was to study the social behavior of the spotted hyena in Kenya. The expedition was run by Dr. Laurence Frank, of Berkeley, and there were twelve of us, including a college-textbook writer, some arrogant Sierra Club people, and several zoology students. Before you go on any Earthwatch you are given explicit do's and don'ts. I came across the briefing for the Kenya Earthwatch the other day, and here's the cautionary part: 'Don't go into water over your knees. Crocodiles like knees. Don't step out of a vehicle in tall grass without reconnoitering first (lions and other animals are well camouflaged). . . . Let your ears play their part when you head for the lavatory tent in the middle of the night, bring a flashlight with you, and never assume that because you were someplace yesterday and it was free of animals, it will apply a day or even hours later.' We'd gather in groups of three or four during the day, and go off in a jeep to find hyenas and record what we saw. Dr. Frank wanted something like 'Cub No. 22 walked twelve metres toward its mother, who picked the cub up in her mouth by the nape of its neck,' and not 'A darling cub ran over and nestled up to its adorable mother.'

"I've been on six Earthwatches. Two were bird trips—one to Panama to find the great black-and-white owl and the oropendola, which has a sharp, crowlike beak and looks like a big oriole, and the other to study cranes in the marsh country up near the Chinese-Mongolian border. In China, there were red-cheeked, lusty, loud people who kept pigs in their front yards, and there were visiting Chinese professors housed in miserable barracks. Captive cranes, five feet tall, were used to attract wild cranes, and the captive cranes lived better than the professors. And I've made two trips to Madagascar with the zoologist Alison Jolly to study ring-tailed lemurs." Daphne wrote an account of her second Madagascar trip for the Bernardsville *News,* which covers the area in New Jersey where she grew up. Parts of it are extremely vivid and are written in a kind of Gilbert White prose:

> We spent several hours along the rainy rain forest paths, admiring ferns and listening to clear parrot whistles. At last four indri appeared in a clearing, tail-less large grey and white lemurs. They ate leaves thoughtfully from thin trees; then with mighty leaps advanced into the forest where they disappeared.
>
> We drove along several noisy metal bridges, past Amboasary village with its Sunday cattle market, over the Mandrare River into dry country, and continued on a long straight road through sisal plantations to the tin-roofed cement building of the Reserve. A dancing band greeted us with fierce lunging and stamping. A guard wearing a pointed little straw Antandroy hat and whistle in his mouth led the gang. He recognized me from the Earthwatchers; he embraced me warmly and invited me to prance off with the band.

An accompanying photograph in the paper shows Daphne laughing and dancing arm in arm with the guard, who is brandishing a spear in his right hand.

Daphne played at the Village Gate that evening with her trio. They were set up in the Terrace Bar, which stretches along the front of the Gate on the ground floor. It is a noisy, uncaring place, full of drop-ins and the curious. People talk a lot, and when the music gets in their way they talk louder. Daphne was on a low dais at the east end of the room, with Eddie Berg to her right and Lyn Christie just behind her. During a single, hour-long set, they played ten numbers, among them two Berg originals entitled "Strange" and "Escapade," an Oscar Pettiford blues, "Honeysuckle Rose," "Misty," and Sonny Rollins's "Doxy." The group has built an impressive repertory. It includes discreetly jazzed-up versions of Bach and Scarlatti and Respighi; such country-and-Western numbers as "King of the Road," "Tennessee Waltz," and "Foggy Mountain Breakdown"; ragtime pieces like the "Pineapple Rag," the "Black and White Rag," and "The Entertainer"; and jazz numbers like "Watermelon Man," "Ballin' the Jack," "Summertime," and "Tea for Two." It is a comfortable, nicely balanced group that swings from the inside and has a pleasant, see-through texture. Daphne's pearly treble figures are offset by Christie's bass, and Berg moves easily between. He is the motor of the group. A fleet admirer of Johnny Smith and Charlie Christian and Django Reinhardt, he is little known in the jazz world and prefers to keep it that way. Daphne plays with regal animation, and when she moves into a difficult ensemble passage or takes a brief improvised solo her jaw muscles flicker. She occasionally hesitates rhythmically, but Berg picks her up, and off they go again.

After the set, Daphne sat at a table and talked. "I think of myself as Miss Harp. I take almost any job that comes along. If I could, I'd work every day. When I don't have a gig, I walk over to Kitty O'Shea's and play there. I like harp playing to be an extension of talking, and I don't like it when I get stuck in a corner or off on a balcony. I do Grand Central and Penn Station and the subway so I can talk to people. I'm partly a manic-depressive, and some days are awful, particularly when I'm tired and haven't had my quota of little naps. But playing lifts me right up and makes me feel good again. So does dancing. I love to dance, and for a time I was a greeter at the Tunnel. I've also worked as a cashier in the five-and-ten. I took the job to see if I was employable, and I was thrilled when I wasn't fired."

The Casualness of It

JACKIE MASON

Here is how the comedian Jackie Mason ended his one-man show at the Brooks Atkinson on a Saturday night in January, 1987. "I never thought I'd be a comedian," he said. "Who expected it when you come from a family of rabbis? I have three brothers who are rabbis to this day, and my father all his life was a rabbi. Everybody was a rabbi in the ancestry of my family. So when my father looked at me as his fourth son, naturally he waited for me to become a rabbi and I wanted to make him proud by following in his footsteps, and I started to deliver sermons, and as I was delivering the sermons I didn't feel honest, so I started to tell a few jokes here and there to make it more palatable for myself, and as the jokes were getting better and better I started to charge a cover and a minimum, and then, as the Gentiles in the area heard about me, more and more Gentiles came to see me. So many Gentiles came that before you knew it there was no room for the Jews. The Jews couldn't get in there. I became the only rabbi with a Gentile congregation." This classic Mason mixture of truth and hyperbole was delivered in his customary medium-heavy Yiddish accent, at high speed, yet conversationally, with a steady underlying chuckle (not always audible in the audience but visible in the half smiles that ducked continually across his face), and with a freshness that belied the twelve hours of monologue he had already delivered on Broadway that week. Mason is short and solid, and affects an international look—well-cut double-breasted blazers, gray pants, and conservative shirts and ties. He has receding, curly grayish hair, alert eyebrows, small Gladstones, and sad, questioning eyes. He is a nimble, flyaway presence onstage. He sema-phores a lot with his hands and arms, and during part of the show becomes a frenzied fencer, underlining what he is saying by cutting and slashing the air with a teacher's long pointer. He is a surpassing mimic. Using a guttural mumble, which somehow flawlessly catches his subjects' speech, he mimics their gaits and postures and manner-isms, and there, floating insanely around the stage, are Al Jolson and Bing Crosby and Alfred Hitchcock and Jimmy Cagney. Mason's mas-terpiece is Ed Sullivan. For several minutes, he pedals rapidly across the stage, sometimes moving forward, sometimes backward, some-times in a circle, all the while pounding his chest with a fist, or wring-ing his hands, cardboarding his shoulders, shooting his head out, and gradually moving faster and faster until he suddenly rockets off the stage. It is contagious rampaging Surrealism. It immediately lifts his show from its purported level of Catskills comedy (which it has never been anyway) to that giddy plane where W. C. Fields and the Marx Brothers sport.

Mason rarely stops talking. He talks as easily and steadily offstage as on. Talking is breathing and exercise and thinking for him. It flexes and exhilarates him, emptying his head and filling it again. It distills what he sees and hears. One day, he talked about himself and how he got to Broadway. He was seated on a hard reproduction-Chinese chair in his ecstatically decorated Murray Hill apartment—gold ceilings, gold wallpaper covered with huge black-and-white flamingos, black furniture, a lot of mirrors, and gold vertical blinds. Mason looked like a sparrow in the Everglades. While he talked, he knitted the hair on the back of his head with his fingers, explaining that such fingerwork helps him concentrate. In the manner of most theatrical performers, who tend to look in more often than out, he kept his eyes half closed.

"My friend Jyll Rosenfeld took me to see a one-man show that Dick Shawn was doing on the Coast," he said. "She had helped me raise money for one of my movies, and she had become my manager. Her grandfather owned movie theatres; her father is a movie distributor. After we'd seen Dick Shawn, she said, 'Why don't we take your show on Broadway?' I said, 'Don't be ridiculous. How can a night-club comedian go on Broadway? My accent would automatically make it lowbrow. They'd write me off as a borscht-belt comedian. If I were a black man with an English accent, they'd think it was profound. But I'm a street-corner character, and Broadway audiences have a hoi-polloi attitude.' Jyll said that it should be a production—have a map on the wall, develop gadgets and gimmicks, call it something like 'The World According to Me.' She said on a Broadway stage I'd look like an art form, because they'd never seen a character like me. I said, 'I don't believe any of it, but I'll go along with it. There's a 1 percent chance it will work.' I got together with a West Coast playwright and he came up with some ideas—have some books onstage, have some chairs, have a wind when I did my weather-forecasting routine. All this would make the production look like something else than a monologue. We opened the show that way at the Las Palmas Theatre in Los Angeles in June of 1986, and after a week I knew it stunk. My style is the casualness of it—just a friend telling his insights about life, about the world. The way we were doing it, it made me an actor. I was doing a role instead of working from the heart. I kept the map and the globe and the locater, but I threw the rest of the affectations out. I started doing the show as a monologuist. I started taking my chances by being myself, and I was afraid it would die. But suddenly it was sensational. Mel Brooks, George Burns, Jane Fonda, Milton Berle, Jimmy Stewart, Kirk Douglas, Alan Alda—everybody came to see me. We moved to the Canon Theatre in Beverly Hills, and Nick Vanoff became a partner. He was excited about taking the show to Broadway. But I still wasn't sure. I had worked at Dangerfield's in New York for four or five years and hadn't been a huge hit, so why would I be a huge hit ten blocks away? We opened on Broadway in December of 1986, and closed a year later so I could go to the Coast and make *Caddyshack II*. We reopened in May of this year. And I'm a star. Just like that.

"I first worked in night clubs in 1961. When I decided to move out from the hotels and bar mitzvahs I had been doing, the bookers told me that I was too Jewish, that even if the Gentiles could understand what I said with my accent they wouldn't like me. I began to realize that what these bookers were doing was transferring their persecution complexes to me. They were putting their guilt, their paranoia, on me. I got a booking in a club in Los Angeles called the Slate Brothers. It was like the Blue Angel in New York—very hip, very smart. The exact opposite of what the bookers feared happened. The audience loved every word I said. I was a smash in five minutes. Then Bill Dana and Jan Murray, who knew Steve Allen, came in, and they got me an audition with Allen. When I arrived at the studio, it was the usual television-studio scene—three people doing something, four people almost doing something, ten people watching them, twelve people looking lost, and thirty people just standing around. I told one joke, and Allen said, 'He's hilarious.' As soon as he said that, my heart dropped. Being on TV was remote and frightening to me. The first show I did with Allen, I was so nervous I didn't even hear myself. I was talking by rote. I didn't know if I did good or bad. I didn't hear any laughs. After, I was bombarded with calls from New York. 'Brilliant!' 'Great!' I went back to the show two weeks later, and I was a big hit again. I went from three hundred to five thousand dollars a week. I went into the Copa as the opening act for Connie Francis. I did Jack Paar and Garry Moore and Ed Sullivan. I became a regular on the Sullivan show.

"Then came the famous finger episode. It was 1964. The show was being cut short that night, because President Lyndon Johnson was making a speech. Sullivan held up two fingers to warn me I had two minutes left, and I held up a hand mimicking him, but, the way I did it, it looked like I was giving him the finger. My God, I was only a few years out of being a rabbi. I didn't even know what such a gesture meant. I had never used dirty jokes or bad language. I still don't. There was an uproar, and Sullivan dropped me. I was suddenly considered obnoxious, arrogant, vulgar, unstable, abnormal. It was a classic instance of being railroaded beyond reparation. I sued Sullivan for breach of contract and defamation of character. Paul O'Dwyer was my lawyer. He was a righteous man, a man of principle. We would have won the case, but my booking agency persuaded me to settle out of court. They argued that it was wrong to win out over Ed Sullivan. He was a national hero, as American as apple pie. It was a stupid decision. You settle out of court, who knows who wins? A fight is fascinating; shaking hands is not. A year later, I ran into Sullivan at the airport, and he apologized. He had studied the films. He had me back on his show, and he apologized on the air. But it served no purpose. The rumor had been built—I was a dirty comedian. My price didn't go down. I still worked the big clubs. People like Merv Griffin were still crazy about me. But it came to me that I was losing certain jobs because of my reputation. I didn't sense myself becoming a major comedian. I was a name, not a star. I still made a good dollar, but not the top dollar.

"In 1969, I did a play on Broadway. I worked on it for six months. Mike Mortman helped me. He was my sounding board, and he knew about writing plays. I ran around and raised money, including my own. The play was called *A Teaspoon Every Four Hours*. It must have had the longest preview run in Broadway history—ninety-seven performances. After every performance, I came out and asked for opinions from the audience. They loved that. It made them feel like philosophers. I also promoted the play on every TV show I did. All this convinced me I had a big hit. The show opened and closed in one day. The critics said it was the worst crap they ever saw. Where does this schlemiel get the idea he's an actor and a playwright? He should go into a different business. And so on. It didn't make me feel too good. But I told myself that life is too short, that you have to keep moving, that you're lucky to be on earth in the position you're in. I don't even have a copy of the play. But I'm looking for one. It might make a good movie."

Mason laughed. "I wish I knew what a good movie is," he said. "I made my first one, called *The Stoolie*, not long after the Broadway disaster. People who did *They Shoot Horses, Don't They?* and *The Karate Kid* were involved. I didn't like the script much, but I thought it would create a new aura around me. It would be like Red Buttons in *Sayonara* and Sinatra in *From Here to Eternity*. It would send shock waves through the country. It opened, and the critics loved it. But nobody came, and the picture died.

"Then I did a TV pilot for a kind of comedy Phil Donahue show, but I could see in the producers' faces that they couldn't care less. They always had some excuse—the curtain is crooked, there are too many shadows in the picture, the people are too old, too thin, too fat. So that went nowhere. The next movie I tried was about a deli owner who looks like a famous atomic scientist. *A Stroke of Genius*, it's called. I acted in it, and I put in a million three of my own money. The picture stunk, the execution stunk. My intelligence seemed to have a hole in it.

Everything I did was caving in. I felt that something was wrong, something was off kilter. I lost some confidence in myself. We reshot it, and it was somewhat better. But it's still in the can. An old friend from yeshiva, Morty Davis, offered me money to try another picture. He was my biggest fan. He'd bring his whole family into Dangerfield's, into the hotels in the mountains. He couldn't understand why I wasn't the world's biggest star. He was like an older brother. The new movie was called *Stiffs*, and it's about three men who inherit a funeral parlor. One is Jewish, one is black, and one is Italian. I was one of the three. I worked very hard, but my lack of confidence made me let other people take over the picture. It didn't come out so hot. It had screenings. It was flat. I reshot it, and screened it again. It was still no good. And there it stands. I went bankrupt on this picture. Before my Broadway show opened, I was broke."

Mason went into the kitchen, a dark mirrored area at the back of the living room, and poured himself a tall glass of orange juice. Then he answered half a dozen phone calls, prefacing each conversation with a fast, double-barrelled "Hellohello!" He finished talking and looked around the room. "I don't know what I need birds on the wall for," he said. "Or all this fancy furniture. I have never been interested in furniture. I told them when they picked out this apartment to fix it how they liked it. This is what they did. Can you believe it? The least they could have is a decent chair. You can do anything here but sit in a comfortable chair. People tell me these things wouldn't happen if I had a wife. I think of marriage like it's football—it's not for me. I enjoy the company of women. I like to experience different relationships. I don't like to be committed to one person. I would never be comfortable in a marriage. People forget about the freedom of choice in such situations. Marriage doesn't suit everybody. People think that everybody should be married. But most people who are shouldn't be. The contract they enter into becomes a fraud, a mockery. Eighty percent of the men who are married cheat, and 50 or 60 percent of the women. Very few married people are happy. I wouldn't say I'm not lonely sometimes, but married people are often lonelier. Why are they always looking for another couple to go out with? Why is it inconceivable that they have a good time just with each other? Married men have said to me, 'What kind of life is that, living in hotels, in little rooms?' I don't get too self-involved. I never sit around immersed in myself. I like to go to the coffee shops and watch people. Every person is a book. The whole world is a performance.

"I idolized my father. I stole my whole personality from him. To me he was the greatest human being on earth. I was born Jacob Maza, in Sheboygan, in 1934. My father was a rabbi there. He and my mother and my three older brothers were born in Russia. They came over in 1930. I was the first in the family to be born here. There were three sisters after me—Susan, Gail, and Evelyn. The older brothers are Joseph and Gabriel and Bernard. All but one of my sisters and brothers live in New York or New Jersey. We are very close. My father looked like me, except for his beard. My mother was a small lady who wore housecoats and only went out to buy food. She was the traditional Jewish wife of the time, totally submissive, always preoccupied with cleaning and cooking, with following us around with soup and a piece of cake. She felt morally obligated to serve her husband and children. She and the women like her felt guilt about ever enjoying themselves. Just resting for a minute was a crime. Her name was Bella, and my father's name was Eli. They were both from Minsk.

"When my father came over from Russia, he discovered there were too many rabbis in New York—that's why he moved us to Sheboygan. Then he discovered that it was impossible to train anyone for the rabbinate in Sheboygan, so after four or five years he brought us back to

New York. There had been many generations of rabbis in my family. Being a rabbi was inviolate, a heritage. It was blasphemous for us to think of being anything else. We moved to the Lower East Side. First to Rutgers Street, then Henry Street, then Madison. The children there spoke English to each other and Yiddish to the parents. My father put things together to make ends meet, but he had a murderous struggle. It was yesterday's bread, secondhand grapes, fourth-rate cherries. We celebrated when we had fresh fruit. My father was still a rabbi, but he also made a living from writing books. He was an interpreter of the Talmud who became a great scholar, an intellectual giant in Orthodox circles. In the halls of a place like a yeshiva, they would know what my father was. But my father never made things easy for himself. He wasn't a good politician, a diplomat. His principles were more important to him than negotiations. He had a spirited concern for the underdog. At the yeshiva, I studied Hebrew and the Talmud. The secular studies were incidental. Then I went to C.C.N.Y. I majored in psychology. I had a B.A. and a certificate to be a rabbi. My first job was in Latrobe, about thirty miles from Pittsburgh. I had a hundred and fifty people in the congregation. I already knew that being a rabbi was not what I wanted. I knew I wasn't as religious as I was supposed to be. The basic message had a severity that didn't reflect my attitudes. I'd preach against the pleasures of the earth, and a beautiful blonde would go by and I'd lose my place. But I didn't want to hurt my father. It was a great source of conflict with me. I was in Latrobe six or seven months. Then I went to Weldon, North Carolina. I was there about as long. I was beginning to feel like I was teaching people to dance when I hated dancing. It was then I made up my mind I couldn't be a hypocrite all my life, that I couldn't personify a character I wasn't.

"So I went to the Catskills to be a social director. The social director in a hotel in the Catskills was supposed to be a tummler, a noisemaker, a court jester. He was supposed to entertain. He was supposed to come up with games and diversions, with bingo nights and movie nights and calisthenics. This was based on the belief that a Jew can never rest, that as soon as a Jew does nothing he complains. All this was very uncomfortable for me. Creating such activities was like starting an earthquake. I didn't see any sense in athletic activity. Can anything be more stupid than skiing? You leave your steam heat to go out in the cold and run up and down a mountain. A miserable experience. I worked as a social director for one season—in about six different places. The bosses would get sick of me when I didn't create enough activity, and I'd move on. But in the playhouse at night I was always a hit. I had learned when I was a rabbi that I could make people laugh. I decided I wanted to see if I could become a professional comedian. I started to play bar mitzvahs, Purim parties, Passover parties, weddings, banquets, fund-raisers—all Jewish-related events. I developed a reputation in the mountains that I was funny, and the next year I went as a comedian to the Catskills. One hundred dollars a show at the Concord Hotel. This was in 1958. With my father, I decided that compassion mattered more than the lies I told him. I created different excuses. I was on vacation, I was this, I was that. I always wore a yarmulke and a hat when I was with him. He never knew I was not a practicing rabbi. He believed me because he wanted to believe me. He was so involved in his religious life he couldn't believe anything else. He thought of me as someone who liked to joke. My brothers knew, but they saw no future for me as a comedian. The idea that someone could be a hit or famous doing what I was doing was too farfetched for them."

Mason's Broadway show has evolved steadily. He estimates that by the end of its first year a third of the first act was new and two-thirds of the second. He is not a standup comedian in the usual sense; he moves too much, and even sits down. Nor is he given to one-liners, although small jokes pop irrepressibly out of him when he is at ease offstage: "A person who speaks good English in New York sounds like a foreigner." Mason is an old-fashioned moralist. He is rarely tasteless or cruel; he is a gentle comedian, in the manner of Bob and Ray or Fred Allen, even though he sometimes shouts for emphasis and uses such flavorful words as "stink" and "bastard" and "schmuck." He constantly eavesdrops on the world around him, and when something provokes him he distills it, adds his own italics, and tries the new routine out on friends in one of the coffee shops he hangs out in during the day. If the routine works, he may insert it in the show, and if it works there he may keep it in. If he keeps it, he will improvise on it until it wears thin, and then drop it.

Mason's show has the pacing and intensity of an old-time musical, and it is always startling to realize after fifteen minutes that there is just one person onstage. He will begin the evening by explaining that you don't need three hundred people to make a show, although that's what Broadway audiences have come to expect. One person is enough— look at Michelangelo, who painted the ceiling of the Sistine Chapel by himself, and took thirty years. After discussing people who need a lot of people, Mason describes a complex visit with a psychiatrist, whom he goes to in hopes of finding out who he is. At the end, the psychiatrist pays Mason for having found out who *he* is. Beverly Hills is next. If you hate people, it's the place to live, because you never see anybody except Japanese gardeners, who have worked there for years without knowing whom they work for. Most of the people who claim they live in Beverly Hills actually live in a place called "adjacent." Most of them also own a Mercedes, Cadillacs being regarded as embarrassing even by Cadillac owners, who claim they would never buy a car made by "those Nazi bastards." A lot of movie producers live in or near Beverly Hills, and the chances are they haven't made a picture in ten years. "All they talk about is where they are going to put the sex scene in their next movie," Mason will say. "They convince themselves that they're not interested in sex for sex's sake, but—let's be honest—since everybody does it movies should reflect reality, which is the essence of truth. [A short pause] That's what they tell you. And I keep wondering [another pause]: everybody also has soup. How come I never see soup in any movie? [His voice rising] More people have soup than sex. [He points to someone in the first couple of rows.] You look to me like you had enough sex. I can tell you're ready for soup. I never heard anybody say, 'I'm too tired, forget the soup.' Does your wife ever say, 'What a headache I got. [He shouts.] Soup is out!'?"

He prefaces a section on international and political matters by pointing out that two-thirds of the world is covered with water, and do we need so much? The Gentiles do, he answers, but the Jews don't, because every Jew has a swimming pool. He goes on to say that individual Jews don't like to fight ("How many times have you heard a Jew say, 'If he says one more word, I'll . . .'?"), but the Israeli Army is so tough it could have taken the Suez Canal, except that the canal has no boardwalk.

Mason has prepared the audience for the longest (and perhaps the best) part of his show, a comparative-anthropology class on the tribal customs of Jews and Gentiles. After explaining how good Gentiles are at building things and how maladroit Jews are, he continues, "A Gentile has a house to live in. A Jew has a house to show it. Why do you think a Gentile doesn't even care if his house flies away in a flood or a thunderstorm or a hurricane? Because they know in two minutes they could put up another house. They put up houses in a second. Watch the seven-o'clock news, every single day throughout the whole Midwest of this country Gentile houses are flying around. They're flying all over the country. Homes are flying, and the same Gentiles are standing there. The same ones!

" 'What happened to your house?'

" 'It left again!'

" 'Why do you live here?'

" 'Because my roots are here!'

" 'Where's your roots?'

" 'It went with the house!'

"It means nothing to them. A minute later, he has another house. Why do you think if a Jewish house gets a nick on it ten seconds later there's nineteen lawyers and fifty accountants? Because it's a different problem for a Jew. See, it's not only Jews. It sounds like I'm singling Jews out. All minorities are struggling for identity. What do you think psychologists mean when they talk about the identity crisis in this country? It's the thing that all minorities suffer from. They always feel left out. They always feel alienated. Because they are. They're always struggling to prove how much money they got. So they have things to show you to give them an identity. Why do you think a Jew buys a boat? Does a Jew like a boat? There's no bigger schmuck on this earth than a Jew with a boat. I know five thousand Jews with boats and I never seen one Jewish boat move yet. Because a Jew hates a boat. He buys the boat to show it to you. 'That's my boat. You saw it? Good! Let's get the hell out of here!' "

He works his way through the attitude of Gentiles toward their bosses (reverence) and the attitude of Jews toward theirs (scorn); through Gentile behavior in restaurants (passive, and they always end up singing "Happy Birthday") and Jewish behavior (a Jew walks in like a partner in the business, and after he has finally found a table he likes he says, "Where is that draft coming from?"); through what Gentiles say to each other when they leave the Jackie Mason show ("Have a drink? How 'bout you? Have a drink?") and what Jews say ("Did you eat yet?").

Mason got another glass of orange juice, and talked about his material. "I write all my own stuff," he said. "I always have. I get ideas from everything I see in life. Like a guy taking twenty minutes to park his car. His wife is with him.

" 'Take it easy,' she says. 'You're going to hit the curb.'

" 'I've parked here a million times,' he says.

" 'See that, you schmuck! You scraped the tire. You ruined the tire!'

" 'How come I never do this when I park alone? You mix me up.'

" 'I never said a word. But it also happens when I'm not here.'

" 'How do you know if you're not here?'

"And so on. I'm still working that up. I'm also working on a caviar routine. I go to this millionaire's house and the first thing he offers me is caviar. He hates caviar, I hate caviar, but the first thing you know we're eating caviar. Neither of us can believe that people would eat something that tastes that bad. We both have to prove that we're caviar people, that we have the status to buy and eat caviar. And so on. Another one I'm working on has to do with foreign cars. The back seat in these cars is so small you have to be thrown in. You have to be a contortionist, an acrobat, a four-year-old midget. Once you're in, you discover it's so narrow you have to sit sideways, and the man who owns the car tells you, 'Who says you have to sit straight in a car? You sit that way, there's no problem.' Except your knee is in your mouth, and if the car hits a bump you fly up to the third floor.

"I don't find performing too intimidating. To walk out on a stage and tell jokes, it's not that rare a trick. Collectively, people react the same way to the same material. But the environment is very important. Sometimes you get an unmanageable situation. This happened to me at a bar mitzvah in Miami a couple of years ago. I started telling jokes, but nobody was listening. The mike was only half working, and everybody was on the other side of the room, screaming. Two hundred people running with a piece of cake in one hand and a cup of coffee in the other. Bar mitzvahs used to be religious occasions, emotional occasions. They used to be touching moments in a family relationship. What did you have at your bar mitzvah? Sponge cake. Now it's: Who did you have at your bar mitzvah? Jackie Mason.

"There are differences in every audience. Some comedians are boring because they aren't in touch with the audience's mind. Onstage, it's as if you were carrying on a conversation with the audience, even though you are doing all the talking. You have to adjust to the reactions of the audience. It's an evolved awareness. Timing is a knowledge and awareness of the mood of an audience. There are performers who bully an audience. I try to involve the audience emotionally in my message. They have to believe what you're saying. You set up a basic premise, and if they are convinced of its truth it becomes a living experience to them, and they are ready to be moved by laughter. Part of being fascinating to an audience is being unpredictable. You have to make them anxious to hear what you say next.

"I'm not a fly-by-night character. My mind is too active. It has too much curiosity, too much concern about the world. My outlook on life will always make me replenish my material. I'm totally unaware of retiring. You don't see ninety-year-old bricklayers and plumbers. But you see ninety-year-old comedians."

Jazz Clubs

MAX GORDON, BARNEY JOSEPHSON AND BRADLEY
CUNNINGHAM

The owners of jazz night clubs have ranged from Capone mobsters to
sleazeballs of various grades to decent men, even outright moralists.
Here are three of the last. They share certain things—all are honest,
all love the music, and all have more or less backed into their line of
work. The first is the venerable and indomitable Max Gordon.

I

He is short and bent and gnomish. His hands and feet are childlike,
and he is dominated by a large head, which in turn is dominated by a
broad brow and heavy white receding hair. His eyes are sad, and prune-
like wrinkles course down his face. (When the comedian Joe Frisco
visited Gordon's first club, the Village Fair Coffee House, in the early
thirties, he pointed to Gordon and asked a friend, "Who's that miserable guy by the door? He looks like the Wailing Wall in Jerusalem.")
But Gordon, like many hesitant, inward-gazing people, glows. His
Solomonlike visage is constantly ruffled by smiles and laughter, and if he
gets excited his voice, which creaks when he breaks one of his occasional

long silences, booms. He is a funny, dreaming man who shrugs off victory and laughs at defeat, and who invariably treats the weaknesses in others with respect. One of his many admirers has said of him, "If I had to spend the rest of my days on a desert island and could take just five people, Max would top the list."

Gordon lives in an airy, high-ceilinged apartment on East Seventy-ninth Street with his wife, Lorraine, and his daughters, Rebecca and Deborah. Gordon talked about his life one morning: "When I came to New York in 1926 I lived in furnished rooms. I must have lived in twenty or more of them, and they were mostly in a complex, a rabbit warren owned by a man named Albert Strunsky. The N.Y.U. Law School is there now. The side facing Washington Square had big studios where fancy people paid seventy-five dollars a month, but we lived on the other side, in rooms with hall toilets, for six dollars a week. There was no central heating, just gas heaters, and you took your life in your hands if you went to sleep in the winter and left the gas on. Strunsky was a marvellous man. He'd known Jack London, and he loved creative people. You could always owe him money. He looked like an Irishman, with his beet face and polished scalp. A cousin, Simeon, was an editorial writer with the *Times*, and another relative, Anna, was a Yiddish writer. I think one of his daughters married Ira Gershwin. Strunsky was always around, and when someone asked him where his beautiful wife was, he'd say, 'Oh, Palm Beach.' I was walking down the street a while ago, and there was an old sofa, all broken down and gaping, sitting by the curb. It made me laugh. It was authentic Strunsky period.

"I'd come to New York from Portland, Oregon, ostensibly to go to Columbia Law School. I was raised in Portland, but I was born in 1903 in Svir in Lithuania. I was the third of four children. My mother brought us over to Providence, Rhode Island, in 1908. My father had already established himself in the dairy and delicatessen business. I remember him churning butter in the window of his shop, and going for rides on Sunday in a surrey with a fringe on top. We spoke Yiddish at home, but my Yiddish fell away. I have no memory of the lack of English. I can't read Yiddish now, although I speak it haltingly, and I probably could enjoy a play in Yiddish. We stayed in Providence several years. Then my father moved to Portland, and we followed him. He became a kind of peddler, and he'd go out to the eastern part of the state and buy furs from trappers. He used a horse and wagon first, and then he had a Ford pickup truck. We were poor, and we hustled as children. I sold papers, and we'd save all kinds of boxes during the year and sell them for people to sit on at the Rose Festival parade. Mark Rothko, the great painter, was related to us, and we sold papers together. We talked about it on the phone the day before he committed suicide, just a little while ago. I couldn't understand him doing that. He had a big studio, a home, money. When I went to the funeral his elder brothers were there, and I asked them why they had let Mark sell papers and run the streets when they already owned a drugstore. They shrugged and said, 'What did we know in those days?' My mother and father were separated off and on when I was growing up. I never knew why. My father worked hard, and he was a good, gentle man. But my mother was hard-bitten. She was not a happy woman. She had a goiter and a heart condition. But she had that Jewish drive to educate her children, and I think I broke her heart when I didn't become a lawyer. When I was in high school I hung around with people who read novels and poetry, and I never studied. But I went to Reed College in Oregon, and when I was a junior I got fed up. I wanted to get away, to lash out, so I matriculated at Stanford and then ran out of money. I got a job in an all-night cigar store, saved some money, and went back to Reed and graduated. I only lasted at Columbia six weeks. I lived on the campus for a while after I'd dropped out, and I got to know the intellectuals, like Gus Solomon, who's a federal judge in Oregon, and Furner Nuhn, who contributed to the *American Mercury*. Then I moved down to Strunsky's. I didn't know what I wanted to do. All I knew was that work was unworthy of me. What *was* worthy I didn't know. So I wouldn't work until I really had to, and then I'd get a job in a mail-order place, running an addressograph machine or licking envelopes. When I tired of one place I'd go to another. Or if I had scraped enough money together I'd lay off a couple of months. I spent my days in the Public Library and my nights at Paul's on Wooster Street or Sam Johnson's on Third Street. I stayed up until three or four in the morning and slept until two or three in the afternoon. Paul's and Sam Johnson's were coffeehouses with poetry. Eli Siegel, who started a movement called Aesthetic Realism, ran Sam Johnson's. He'd won the *Nation* poetry prize in 1925 for 'Hot Afternoons Have Been in Montana.' There would be poetry readings and lots of discussion groups, and I met people like Joe Gould and John Rose Gildea and Harry Kemp and Max Bodenheim, whom I'd read in college. There was a lot of drinking—wine, or alcohol mixed with the essence of juniper. It was Prohibition that did that. The minute repeal came, everybody went on the wagon. Gildea was a wonderful man. He married an East Side girl, and he'd come to the Village in tails and stay three days. He improvised poetry for drinks, and some of it was marvellous. I don't think he ever published anything. I remember walking him home under the Sixth Avenue 'L' on a freezing winter night while he spouted this great poetry at the top of his lungs. I took Joe Gould home, too. Malcolm Cowley would give him piles of books to review, but he read very fast, skipping a lot, and his reviews were short and sketchy. Harry Kemp, whose poems you can find in the old anthologies, was a huge, heavyweight strapping guy. A big, real, impossible man. He'd had an affair with

Upton Sinclair's wife, and in 1922 he published *Tramping on Life*, a very successful autobiography. He followed it with *More Miles*, but that flopped. He ran Harry Kemp's One-Act Playhouse, where Clifford Odets started as an actor. Kemp lived on the dunes at Provincetown, and he helped start the Provincetown Playhouse. When he came back to town he'd look for me in the coffeehouses and he'd shout, 'Max! Where are you? I have a new poem to read to you!' and crush me with an embrace. I was enchanted with Provincetown when I went up there in the thirties. Kemp would roar down Commercial Street, talking, talking, talking, and it was like the Village, only with water."

Gordon went out to the kitchen and made a pot of tea. "I'm not much at this sort of thing," he said when he came back, "but it's real tea and it's hot." He lit a big cigar. It made him look top-heavy. He puffed for a while, his eyes narrowed against the smoke, and then put the cigar down and took a sip of tea.

"In 1929 I went home. It was frustration and fatigue, and I went home to recharge my batteries. I stayed four or five months and came back in November of that year and drifted into my old life of odd jobs with mail-order outfits and writing for little puff magazines. By this time I had vague visions of being a writer. For the puff magazines, which were a racket, we'd pick out people of the second and third echelon who had been in the news and write congratulatory biographies, about three hundred words or so, and then call them up and read them what we'd written and ask them how many copies they wanted at thirty-five cents a throw. I also wrote a humorous essay which had to do with a *schnorrer*, a Yiddish word for a phony promoter. It was printed in the *Menorah Journal*, which was edited by Eliott Cohen, who later edited *Commentary*. Albert Halper, the novelist, was in the same issue, and I noticed a while ago that he's just published an autobiography. I knew I wasn't a writer, but I also knew I had to be *something*. I had got to the point where I was sick worrying about my mother, about what she was thinking of me. People didn't have contempt for their parents then, and this guilt was engulfing me. Ann Andreas, who was a good friend of mine, saved me. She suggested I start a decent coffeehouse, since Sam Johnson's and Paul's had gone downhill. My sister had moved to New York, and between us we raised four or five hundred dollars. I found a half basement on Sullivan Street that seated about seventy-five. I think it's a fraternity house now. We opened in the latter part of 1932, and we called it the Village Fair Coffee House. We served tea and coffee and sandwiches and setups. The waitresses wore pajama-type pants, and it was the sort of place where they'd sit and talk with the customers if they were invited to. But it was all very innocent. The poets, who were always looking for new places, started coming in, and I hired Ivan Black, the press agent, as a master of ceremonies and a bouncer. I fed him and give him five bucks a week, and he organized everything. He was a newspaperman and a poet and he read his own stuff, including a risqué parody of Joyce and Gertrude Stein that had run in *Transition*. I came across a reprint of it the other day in an old file, and, you know, it's pretty funny. It's called 'Mister Weirdy at Home.'"

Gordon shuffled some papers, cleared his throat, and read aloud:

At that time he was constipaching, ins aferment outs abloat, his face-skin a ptomaine green Oily. He was about to write his gratest poem. Pianowing was his livelihoodway and even more his lifeleewayhoot but when he got leadbelly he verscript. He put on a Beethovenfrown as browclasp. He dipt his pen and poised.

Gordon laughed. "It really went over big, and when he'd finish, Ivan would call on poets in the audience to read. They'd get food or liquor or fifty cents. Graham Norwell, a Canadian painter, did the murals in the place. He was a wonderful, handsome man, but he'd lost his teeth and he was a drunk. I paid him in gin. Once, when he had an exhibition of his stuff over in Brooklyn, he went to the opening, and he looked so awful—I think he'd dyed his hair orange—that they wouldn't let him in. We had other entertainment besides the poets. The late Michael Field's wife danced to records, and so did the painter Oronzo Gasparro. Maggie Egri sang Hungarian folk songs that she said she had learned at her mother's breast in Joplin, Missouri. She was a real, bona-fide witch. I used to stand on the side and wonder what it all meant, and yet in a way I was part of it, too. After a while, things got sort of drunken and evil-seeming. Uptown people started coming down so they could say they'd bought John Rose Gildea a drink, and a lot of the poets became more interested in the bottle than they were in conversations about life and literature. Then, unbeknownst to me, one of the waitresses got caught trying to sell liquor to a cop in plain-clothes, so they put a cop on the premises every night, and there he sat in his uniform, and it put a pall on the place. I could have given him twenty-five dollars and he would have gone away, but I didn't know enough. The place had been jammed every night, but in a month's time it was empty, and we closed. We'd been running a year."

Gordon stood up, cigar in mouth, and stretched. "I've got to get down to the club. There are some orders coming in, and my day porter is sick. The old Charles on Sixth Avenue serves a pretty good lunch." Ten minutes later he reappeared, housed in a dark suit and a lively tie. He walked to Park Avenue and found a cab.

"I was out of work for a while," Gordon said. "Then I put in six weeks running a place for a mob underling named Frankie Starch. He wasn't doing any business in the place he had, and he asked me to come in as a partner at thirty-five dollars a week. I changed the name of the place to the Village Fair Coffee House, and all the same poets and painters appeared. But it wasn't the same, because Starch and his friends were always around. I couldn't handle them. They were a tough bunch, and Starch kept referring to the poets as 'creeps.' I was eating in an all-night cafeteria after work one night and one of his hunkies found me and said, 'Frankie wants to see you.' Oh, boy, I thought. But all he wanted was to fire me, which he did. The last time I saw him, years ago, he was running a newsstand on Sixth Avenue and Third Street. I'd saved a hundred and fifty dollars, and I borrowed another fifty from a friend at Columbia, and in February of 1934 I found another basement place, at 1 Charles Street. Jack Delaney, the Village pub keeper, had had it one time, and I rented it for twenty-five dollars a month. It didn't have a stick of furniture, but I knew Frances Bell, from Provincetown. She had a place up there called the White Whale, and she had another one in an old blacksmith shop on Barrow Street. It had brick walls and belly stoves and it was so cold that winter—the temperature hit twenty below in New York—you couldn't pick up the silver. She gave me a bunch of barrels—big ones to stretch planks between for tables, and smaller ones to sit on—and I gave her a due bill for seventy-five dollars. I can't remember why, but I called the place the Village Vanguard, and a lot of the old crowd, including Gasparro and Maggie Egri and such, came back. After a year or so we moved, not losing a night's business, to the present Vanguard. It had been a speak called the Triangle Gardens. It was bigger—I could only seat forty or fifty at the old place—and it seemed to me that moving there would be like growing up. Then the damnedest thing happened, and it really shook me up. I got arrested and spent a night in jail. Someone had written obscene graffiti on the men's-room wall, and there is a crazy New York ordinance that holds a cabaret owner responsible for such things. I had to go to court in a paddy wagon, and when the judge heard from the cop why I'd been arrested and that I'd spent the night in jail, *he* was astonished and dismissed the case. But I've never forgotten the experience. There must be twenty coats of paint on the bathroom walls at the club, and the only things I don't wash off or paint over are scribblings like the one I found the other day: 'Roland Kirk is a nice cat.' "

Gordon ordered a Scotch-and-soda at the Charles, which is spacious and plush and emblazoned with paintings of nudes. He settled back and waved his hands in front of him. "This place always reminds me of one of my worst disasters—a fancy ice-cream parlor I opened in 1955 on Fifty-eighth Street near the Paris Theatre. My partner was Michael Field, and we called it Maxfield. The name was almost the only good thing about it. Michael had been a pianist before he got into his cooking school and his cookbooks, and he was a friend from the old days. The idea for the place was mine, and Michael was crazy about it. I wanted a place that would maybe cost ten thousand and that *looked* genuine, but he wanted it to *be* genuine. So we put in a mosaic floor, like the one in the men's room in Penn Station. We found an old Mazda-bulb sign for outside. All the tables and the counter top were marble. I think it took fourteen men to lift that counter into place. The chairs were old ice-cream-parlor chairs, the walls were red velvet and had hand-carved figures on the moldings, and the chandeliers were brass. It was a beautiful place, and it had beautiful food. Michael insisted we make our own ice cream, and he made all the desserts. I never saw so much cream in my life. But beauty is skin-deep, and underneath everything was wrong. We'd spent thousands and thousands and thousands. The floor alone cost thirty-five hundred and the sign twelve hundred, and all that marble was real. Those genuwine ice-cream-parlor chairs were so uncomfortable you couldn't sit in them for more than twenty minutes. We'd found these old glasses for the ice cream in a place down in the Bowery, but they were so heavy you could barely lift them, and they were so big they wouldn't fit into the dish-washer until we had special trays built. The prices were too high. People came around from Bergdorf's for a cup of coffee—*fresh* coffee, never more than twenty minutes old—and it would cost them twenty-five cents, and they'd hit the ceiling. We stayed open until one or two in the morning trying to catch the late crowd, but we didn't have a liquor license. And then the union started giving us trouble. It turned out that I had to run the place because Michael was so busy with his other interests, and at the time I had the Vanguard *and* the Blue Angel to worry about. I'd get to Maxfields at ten every morning absolutely pooped. I told Michael I couldn't put so much time in, and he said he couldn't spare any more, and shortly afterward he walked out and I never saw him again. The place is a Shelley's luncheonette now."

Gordon downed a second Scotch, neat, and ordered bay scallops. "My other great disaster took place ten years before, and the only difference was that it happened on *East* Fifty-eighth Street. Barney Josephson's Café Society Uptown had started doing poorly, and Herbert Jacoby and I bought it from him for seventy-five thousand, renamed it Le Directoire, tossed everything out, redecorated, and maybe spent another seventy thousand. At first it went like a house afire. We had Kay Thompson and the Williams Brothers, and there were literally lines around the block every night. But she left, and Abe Burrows came in, then Pearl Bailey, then Mata and Hari, and every-thing changed. We charged so much money that people got mad and stayed away, and the reason we charged so much was that when we redecorated we had somehow managed to reduce the seating capacity from three hundred and fifty to one hundred and thirty-six. Business got worse and worse, and finally, after eight months, we gave the place back to Barney for five thousand and got out. We'd poured everything from the Blue Angel into it, and it's a wonder that didn't fold, too."

Gordon speared some scallops with his fork and pushed them through his tartar sauce. "The food isn't bad in this old place. These are honest-to-God bay scallops, not the chopped-up haddock that you get most places. At the time of Le Directoire, Jacoby and I had already been in business five years at the Blue Angel, which was on Fifty-fifth between Third and Lexington. He had managed the Ruban Bleu before that, but there was some sort of ruckus and he had walked out. He started coming down to the Vanguard to watch the acts, and we talked. He wanted to open a place, but he didn't have any money, and he asked me to come in as a partner. I put down five thousand, and he borrowed five thousand. It was a strange relationship. Jacoby had run places in Paris, and I guess he had more to do than anyone else with establishing the supper club over here. He's a man of taste and some background and he's also a snob, but I was just a downtown Village boy who got dressed up to go uptown. So at first I had to defer to him in many ways. He did the emceeing, at which he was good, and he did the booking, which tended to follow a delicate, almost esoteric line. The very first show included a French singer, Madame Claude Alphand, and an Ecuadorian baritone, who was terrible, and Sylvia Marlowe, the harpsichordist. The décor reflected Jacoby, too, with its gray velvet walls and rosettes and pink crystal chandeliers. And so did the food. We had a French chef, our own pastries, and Mme. Romaine, the omelette lady, came in every night to cook omelettes for supper. I don't know whether it was ego or what, but as time went on I started making booking suggestions, and it turned out that we tended to agree on most acts. We held auditions one afternoon a week, and eventually the Blue Angel had such a reputation that anyone who had worked there could get a job in any room in the country. In fact, there were acts who'd say they had worked with us when they hadn't, and we'd get verifying calls from bookers and club owners all over the country.

"It's hard to believe now some of the people who worked at the Blue Angel, the acts we helped start off—Josephine Premice, the dancer, and comedians like Kaye Ballard and Carol Burnett and Alice Pearce and Wally Cox and Orson Bean and Phyllis Diller and Shelley Berman. Woody Allen, too, who was so nervous when he started he shook like a leaf, and Nichols and May. There were dozens of singers. Some were established, like Mildred Bailey and Maxine Sullivan, but most were starters, like Andy Williams and the Inca Trio, which had that fantastic soprano, Yma Sumac, and Martha Wright and Pearl Bailey and Bobby Short and Harry Belafonte and Barbra Streisand. Jacoby doted on French acts, and there were nights at the Blue Angel when I never heard a word of English. Irene Bordoni was an oo-la-la French singer and Odette Myrtil was a French comedienne, and there was an amazing act, Les Mains d'Yves Joly, who used their fingers as puppets. There were a lot of English comedians, and one, Douglas Byng, was nerve-racking. He kept twitching his head and looking at his shoulder, as if some sort of bird was sitting there, and he talked so fast I couldn't understand a word. And, of course, there were a great many people— and this is one of the sad things about show business—who performed and did nothing and disappeared. The Blue Angel was a quality room, and we did a good business until we began to feel the pressure from television, in the late fifties. Business dropped off, as it did everywhere. Jacoby got restless, anxious. He wanted to turn the place into a full-time restaurant. We dickered, and I found some buyers from Chicago who were interested in taking over his share, but he couldn't make up his mind, and finally I bought him out for fifteen thousand in cash and a twenty-thousand-dollar mortgage. I changed the acts a little, bringing in Nipsy Russell and Clara Ward, the gospel singer, and Max Morath, the ragtime pianist. But everything looked musty and dusty to me. I couldn't stand the rosettes on the walls, and the floor had got tacky. We were doing fairly well, but the place needed new blood, a new face. After a year or so I said the hell with it, and in the spring of 1964 I sold the works to the Living Room people. It was time for me to go back downtown where I belonged. I'd been neglecting the Vanguard and it wasn't doing well."

Gordon lit a cigar, and walked over to the Vanguard. It is in the basement of a triangular, two-story building that faces Seventh Avenue and is wedged between Eleventh Street and Waverly Place. The door needs paint, and the awning is tattered and worn. It's the sort of entranceway you could pass at an amble and miss. Gordon went down narrow, steep stairs and under a low arch that has probably cracked some of the most distinguished heads in the world. The main room of the Vanguard is, like the building it is in, triangular, and is fifty or sixty feet long. At its apex there is a small bandstand, and its base is flanked by a coatroom and the bar. Behind the bar are the washrooms and a small kitchen. Banquettes line the walls of the main room, and there are a dozen tiny tables. The place didn't look like the Hollywood version of an empty night club. The chairs, instead of being stacked upside down on the tables, were exactly where their last occupants had left them, and the floor was littered with cigarette butts. It was cold, and the room smelled like a cave.

"I've got to get someone in here to clean up," Gordon said. "I never get spooked when I'm here alone, but I can't stand the cold." He turned on a small gas heater by the bandstand, and we went into the kitchen. It was clean and compact, with two big black stoves, a sink, a work-table, a small wooden desk, and a couple of chairs. Gordon sat down at his desk in his hat and coat and made a couple of telephone calls. "My office, my home, my palace," he said when he had finished. "This place has been like a love match to me. I've probably spent more time in it than anywhere else. I've even slept here, stretched out on a couple of tables. I've learned that if you're good to the Vanguard, the Vanguard will be good to you. And I learned that when we moved here. The entertainment then was pretty much catch-as-catch-can. Ivan Black had taken a job over at the Four Trees, which later became Café Society Downtown, and Eli Siegel replaced him as master of ceremonies. He never drank, so I had to pay him, and he recited Vachel Lindsay at the top of his voice. He wasn't everybody's favorite, but he kept things in hand. In between poetry readings I played a phonograph for dancing, and we had a lot of itinerant entertainers. They floated all over the village—operatic baritones, comedians, piano players—and they'd come in and perform and people threw money at them. On Christmas Eves the Almanac Singers would come in and everybody would join them singing. Pete Seeger and Woody Guthrie were in that group. I began to look for acts to put in, and what I wanted was something that would comment on the social and political scene. There was a girl who used to hang around at this time, and her name was Judy Tuvim, which is Hebrew for 'holiday.' She was answering telephones with Orson Welles's Mercury Theatre. She brought down Adolph Green, and he brought in Betty Comden, who was a student at N.Y.U. They were part of a group that had been rehearsing uptown called Six and Company, and I hired them for Sunday nights for twenty-five or thirty dollars. They did a lot of topical stuff, like our selling the Sixth Avenue 'L' to the Japs so that they could make bombs to blow up the Chinese with. They changed their name to the Revuers, and they were so good that the whole town started knocking at the Vanguard door. It got so crowded people had to sit on the floor. So they began performing six nights a week, and they were with me a year. I could have kept them five years, but they were offered more money by the Rainbow Room, and it was a step up for them. They spawned a lot of imitators, but none had that same fresh young quality, that quickness and sparkle.

Folk singers started getting big, and Josh White and Leadbelly came in as a team, and I had Burl Ives and Richard Dyer Bennett and Pete Seeger. I also began hiring jazz groups, like a marvellous trio with Zutty Singleton and Eddie Heywood and Albert Nicholas. I had calypso groups, and Professor Irwin Corey, the comic, first came in 1945. And, by God, he was back with me last week. By this time the Blue Angel was going strong, so we began trying out acts here first and then sending them uptown. That happened with Eartha Kitt and Pearl Bailey and Josephine Premice and Harry Belafonte. Eddie Heywood had brought Pearl Bailey to me, which was often the way I got my best acts, like Aretha Franklin, who was brought here by Major Holley, the bassist. Pearl was a band singer, but she was already doing her thing of switching from singing to talking in the middle of a number, and I encouraged her to do it. I had established a room that was free and easy, and I think *she* felt free and easy. Then somewhere in 1957 I switched almost completely to a jazz policy, even though I still had acts like the Kingston Trio and Mort Sahl and Nina Simone and Miriam Makeba and Lenny Bruce. I never *did* get completely used to Bruce. The four-letter words stuck to me like burrs, the way they still do when I find them on the printed page."

There was a banging at the street door. "That'll be the Coca-Cola man," Gordon said. "I have to let him in. The door upstairs never used to be locked, and people would wander in all afternoon—singers, comics, musicians, looking for jobs. But I got mugged on the stairs about a year and a half ago, so I keep it locked now." Gordon returned, and there was a tremendous *thump-thump-thump* as the delivery man eased his dolly down the stairs. Gordon paid him in cash and sat down.

"I probably have the smallest staff of any place this size in New York. My bartender has been with me twenty years, and there's my day porter. I have a couple of waiters who come and go, and my sister Sadye helps out. She'll be in in a while, so that I can go uptown for a nap. People sometimes ask me who decorated the place. The answer is nobody. It decorated itself. It hasn't changed much. The stage used to be where the bar is now, and a Refregier protégé did the original murals. I remember a horse playing a piano. But the walls crumbled, and the murals with them. People don't seem to care much about eating in basements, so the food end has never been very important. The most ambitious I ever got was when I hired a chef who said he'd studied cooking in Paris. I auditioned him by bringing five or six friends down, and he cooked a beautiful meal. I bought a whole bunch of those utensils for eating snails with and special bowls for onion soup. All that stuff is still packed away in here somewhere. His first night, fifty or so people ordered dinner. The orders kept coming into the kitchen, but nothing came out. The waiters stood around, and when the food was finally ready it was either overdone or underdone or cold. He didn't know what the hell he was doing, but when dinner was over, out he went into the room in his chef's garb, perspiring and covered with gravy stains, and said, 'Well, how was everything, folks?'

"The worst time for the Vanguard came in the early sixties. I had to sell our car and the little place we had built out on Fire Island. One of my girls was there visiting a friend last summer, and they went by our old house and the friend told her it's still called 'the Gordon house.' One of the axioms of the night-club business is that you have to have somebody to lean on for money. Like the man who lent me the fifty dollars to open the first Vanguard in 1934. He lent me ten thousand during the bad days in the sixties, and a week ago I paid him the last fifty dollars. I've never been much of a businessman, but we've taken in some money at times. When I could still afford Miles Davis, he'd bring in nine thousand a week. Money is a funny thing. A lot of musicians have borrowed from me—twenty-five, fifty, a hundred—and most of them pay it back. The ones who don't, though, will pay me, say, half, and then usually I don't see them for a long time. When they show up again, I think, he still owes me twenty bucks, but I don't say anything and he doesn't say anything, and after a while the unpaid money just seems to disappear, as though it had never existed. It's amazing how money can vanish like that. Business has picked up in the last year or so. The kids are coming in, and they aren't so different from the way we were in the late twenties. And I get a lot of blacks, so I only use strong black acts like Elvin Jones and Roland Kirk and Pharaoh Saunders. And the Thad Jones–Mel Lewis big band is in its sixth year of Monday nights. They jam the place, they keep me going. A lot of people sit in, like Ray Charles, when he's around, and last week there were so many visiting musicians in this kitchen I could hardly get in the door. It's like the old jam sessions Harry Lim ran here one night a week in the forties. Of course, I'll never retire. How could I? I couldn't live on Social Security. When my present lease is up, I'll renew it for another ten years."

There were steps on the stairs. "That'll be Sadye now," Gordon said.

In 1980 Max Gordon celebrated his staying power (the Vanguard may be the oldest night club in the world) by publishing a remarkable auto-biography called *Live at the Village Vanguard*. The dust jacket starts the book off just right. A sepia montage photograph shows Gordon stand-ing in front of the Vanguard surrounded by a crowd of his performers. Some are playing instruments (John Coltraine, Miles Davis, Percy Heath, Gerry Mulligan), one is singing (Leadbelly), some are smiling wildly (Coleman Hawkins, Dexter Gordon, Keith Jarrett), some are looking supercilious (Woody Guthrie, Milt Jackson), and one is gazing into the middle distance (Dizzy Gillespie). No one is looking at Gordon. Inside, Gordon threads his way through his life, which must sometimes seem like a montage to him, in a highly original way. The book, which he wrote sheet by careful sheet over a period of seven years, is not a cascade of names (many of his graduates are not mentioned) but a series of sharp, funny dialogues between him and various interlocutors, some real and some distillations of people he has known. Gordon's literary dynamics are startling. He is gentle and poetic, he drones, he is almost ribald. He talks to Joe Glaser, the tough booking agent who made Louis Armstrong a millionaire:

[Dinah Washington] came out of the dressing room into the spotlight and as the applause died down and she was about to go into her opening number, I noticed that she was wearing a blond wig. I couldn't believe it. . . . Nobody laughed, but that was only because of the innate good taste of the Village Vanguard audiences. I told Joe that I was so upset by this vision of a blond wig on Dinah Washington's head that I had to see him. . . .

"A blond wig!" shouted Joe.

"Yes, a blond wig!" I shouted back. "Here's a handsome black woman, a great singer, a star, and she comes out—I didn't believe my eyes—with a blond wig sitting on top of her head."

"These *schwarzes* are nuts," said Joe. "She's got herself a new guy; that's what it is. Otherwise why should she put a blond wig on her head? She's got a new guy taking her money. Let me give you some advice, Max. Don't pay it any attention. Make believe you don't see it. She'll get over it. I know Dinah.

"She'll dump this guy, whoever he is. And the blond wig will go away. As long as business holds up, what've you got to worry about? And, another thing, you think it's undignified, you think it's grotesque. But I'll bet you some fancy customers are quietly getting a kick out of the sight of a blond wig on a black broad."

And he talks to a customer he calls Jim:

"Like I'm telling you, if you'd signed them in the beginning when they came to you; all those acts, unknown, unemployed, raw, hungry acts—if you'd got a piece of the action right in the beginning—then, when they got to be stars, celebrities, you'd be on easy street today, collecting 10 percent of their paychecks and living like a king. Know what I mean?"

It was my friend Jim talking. I hadn't seen him in twenty years. He made a fortune in plastics. He used to be a regular when he was a student at N.Y.U. and Wally Cox was working at the Vanguard . . . I remember he was crazy about Wally Cox.

"Look at the names you found, or they found you—what'd it matter? . . . You turned 'em into stars! You made 'em famous! But what good did it do you? You didn't have a piece of the action.

"All right, you paid Wally peanuts. You thought you were getting a bargain. When he graduated from your joint and went on television, when he was cast as Mr. Peepers in that television series that ran for years, you were left out in the cold. Why? Because you didn't sign him up at the start, when he was still an unknown and needed you."

Jim had a way of worrying me.

"It wasn't so easy," I said to Jim.

Here is Gordon talking to Miles Davis:

Miles didn't coddle his audiences, or his boss either. "You talk, 'Man, this, man that!' " he once growled at me. "Don't talk to me like a black man. You're a white man and don't forget it."

I was in his house on West Seventy-seventh Street. Miles, neat, immaculate, in a tailored suit, dark glasses, asked me, "Did you go up to see my tailor like I told you?"

"Who can afford three hundred for a suit?"

"You're too goddamn cheap."

"If I was making the kind of money I'm paying you, I'd get myself one."

The Baroness Nica Koenigswarter stops in at the Vanguard and talks to Gordon in the kitchen, which is furnished with towering stacks of Heineken's beer, box after box of waiters' checks, a wall clock, photographs, and two dog-eared journals, one to record reservations and one to record the musicians signed up for the coming six months:

> "Darling," the Baroness was saying to me, "you can thank me that Thelonious was on time tonight. If I hadn't driven him down, he'd still be on Sixty-fifth Street waving for a cab. Cabs won't stop for him. They're afraid of him, a big black man gesturing wildly on the corner."

Gordon speculates on the failure of the Blue Angel:

> But there it was, happening all around me. I didn't see it, didn't want to see it—that a new generation of night prowlers didn't want to go to the kind of place the Blue Angel was. They didn't want to watch an act; they wanted to do their own act. They didn't want to sit glued to a chair in a nightclub. They wanted to do their "own thing," investigate the mystery of the night, listen to a little music, get up and dance maybe, or just sit and talk to the girl sitting next to them at the bar.

A week before *Live at the Village Vanguard* was published, Gordon had dinner at La Tulipe with his friend Jim, who was in town for a visit. La Tulipe is the small, first-class French restaurant that was opened on West Thirteenth Street a year and a half ago by John and Sally Darr, who are old acquaintances of Gordon's. Gordon was dressed in his winter uniform: a chocolate corduroy suit, a yellow flannel shirt, long johns, Wallabees, and a black fedora with its brim down. He has become about the size and shape of a Seckel pear. White hair curtains the back of his bare head, and bumperlike black-rimmed glasses shield the front. He walks slowly and sparingly, his feet making parentheses. When he puts on his overcoat and pulls down his black hat, he disappears. Gordon and Jim arrived at La Tulipe at six-thirty and sat down in the tiny bar by the front door. Jim has red hair and is twice the size of Gordon, and he idolizes him. "Max," he has said to Gordon, "you are one of the wonders of New York life." Gordon ordered a half bottle of Chablis, and introduced Jim to John Darr, a bespectacled former headmaster who looks like a former headmaster.

"It's cold in here," Gordon said to Jim. "I don't know, I have this cough and I haven't been feeling all that well lately. But I haven't had a cigar today and I'm not going to have one."

"You should give them up, Max," Jim said. "They'll stunt your growth."

Darr asked Gordon if he'd like to move to his table, and the two men followed him down a short hall and into the dining room, which is medium-sized and plum-colored. "It's cold in here, too," Gordon said. "It feels like the Vanguard before I turn on the gas heaters."

"Those heaters should have gone out with Hoover, Max," Jim said.

Gordon looked at the menu—and the prices—a long time, and shook his head. "And to think I used to eat Sally Darr's cooking free in her apartment." Gordon and Jim settled on tongue päté, sweetbreads (Gordon), red snapper steamed in paper (Jim), and an apricot soufflé. Gordon ordered a bottle of Spanna.

"Max, you wrote a book," Jim said, as if he were complimenting him on catching a huge fish. "When did you get time to write books? During intermission? Who's your ghost?"

"Me!" Gordon said, laughing. Then he leaned back and opened his eyes and mouth, making three big O's. "I started the book around the time Charlie Mingus published his autobiography, *Beneath the Underdog.*

That was seven or eight years ago. In fact, I started it with Nel King, who did Mingus's book with him. She talked to me and wrote a chapter, and on the basis of that chapter she sold the book to Peggy Brooks at Coward-McCann. But when I read what she'd done I hated it. It wasn't me. So Peggy Brooks got Sy Krim, and he taped me and did a chapter, and it wasn't any better. Sy said, 'Max, you gotta write it yourself.' So I began to write. I'd get up at six or seven and have breakfast and write four or five hours. I had a wonderful time. I'd sit there and laugh and knock myself out. But I discovered I had to rewrite everything four times to make it sound like it was only written once. So I rewrote and rewrote—always in longhand on yellow legal pads—and eventually I got a little help from a free-lance editor named Judy Murphy. I kept trying to find a way to get my ideas across, and I hit on dialogues, sometimes with real people, sometimes with people based on real people. Some of the dialogues are fictional, but it's fiction borrowed directly from life. Life fiction, you might call it. And I wanted to make the book a New York book, which it is. It celebrates New York. When I got enough of it in what I considered decent shape, I sent a few chapters around—to Pete Hamill and Nat Hentoff—and the *Village Voice* ran excerpts from them. I got an agent, who wanted to do this and that. One of the thats was Doubleday, which took six months to turn the book down. The manuscript went to Coward-McCann. Peggy Brooks had left, and I'd given my two-thousand-dollar advance to Nel King, who died. Coward-McCann turned it down. Then Marcia Markland at St. Martin's saw the chapters in the *Voice* and called me. I didn't pay any attention at first, but then I did, and we have a book. I'm surprised it came out so well. I really like the chapter on going to Russia with the Thad Jones–Mel Lewis band, and I like the chapters on Lenny Bruce and Richard Dyer-Bennet and the early days with Eli Siegel. People have told me they love the book. I hope they're telling the truth. I've also heard from people who aren't in the book, like Katie O'Brien, a Martha Graham dancer who worked for me forty-four years ago. She said the book was too short. But I never got to know a lot of the people who appeared at the Vanguard. Maybe they were scared of me, maybe I was scared of them. Maybe they were like John Coltrane, who was always surrounded by worshippers. I loved his music, but I never said four words to him."

Gordon picked at his sweetbreads, and Jim tore into his snapper, which he said was superb. The dining room had filled up and warmed up, and Gordon said he was comfortable. Sally Darr, attractive in whites, came out of the kitchen to say hello to Max, and Max asked her who the famous comedian had been at one of the dinner parties he'd attended at her house. He said he'd been trying to think of his name for a week. Did he mean Danny Kaye, she asked. Gordon laughed, slapped the table, and made three O's. Mrs. Darr told the men to enjoy their dinner and said the soufflé would be ready in twenty minutes. Gordon told Jim that his life had changed since he'd last seen him. He said that he and his wife, Lorraine, were separated, and that his daughters, Deborah and Rebecca, were grownup and working. "I live alone in a one-bedroom at Fifth Avenue and Eleventh," Gordon said. "Lorraine and I have dinner every so often, and a couple of summers ago we rented a house out at Three Mile Harbor, on the Island. I have all these little habits that keep me company, and I don't know where they came from. When I get up in the morning, I have a glass of lemon juice and hot water, and half a grapefruit. Then I have two cups of coffee—one with cream and one with boiled milk, half and half. Sometimes I make a little oatmeal, too. I read the *Times* from cover to cover. I'm always reading a book. I don't like modern novels, but I just reread *War and Peace*. What a fantastic, beautiful book! Later in the morning, I might take a nap. Then I have lunch. Sometimes I eat with someone in a restaurant, but not often. Generally, I eat at counters, because I'm alone and you have company at counters. I go to a little place and have steamed milk and honey, or to another place for fruit and cheese. If I want a glass of wine, I go to One Fifth Avenue. After lunch, I go to the Vanguard and put everything in order—phone calls and publicity and liquor orders and booking, and the like. The phone rings every couple of minutes. I've never been able to find anyone who would run the Vanguard the way I do, so I do it myself. Anyway, I'll never sell it. When and if the time comes, I'll give it away. After I've finished my business at the club, around five-thirty, I have another little nap, and go out for dinner—at Joe's, on MacDougal Street, or at Pirandello, on Washington Place. I'm an old face at both places, and that's what I like—to go to places where I'm known. On almost any street in the Village, which *is* a village, someone recognizes me. When I take a little walk Sunday afternoons, I'll stop at the Spring Street Bar and have a glass of wine or some espresso, and the man at the bar knows me and serves me espresso right there. If I go to Bradley's or the Cedar Bar, it's the same—someone knows you and you feel like you're in a small town. After dinner, I go back to the Vanguard and stay until midnight. The old days, I used to walk out of there sweating and exhausted at 4 A.M. I don't have much of a social life anymore. I don't have the time, and I suppose it's different since Lorraine and I aren't together."

Gordon told Jim to eat all the apricot soufflé himself, and Jim did and said it was the best dessert he'd ever had. Jim asked Gordon how his sister Sadye was.

"Funny you should ask," Gordon said. "She gave me quite a scare this week. Sadye's two years younger than I am, and we're very close. She lives by herself up near the George Washington Bridge, but we talk almost every day. I worry about her being alone, because she's inclined to take falls, you know. Anyway, when I called her this past Tuesday the phone rang and rang: no answer. I called back every fifteen minutes for an hour, an hour and a half. The same. I called one more time. Still the same. I got panicky. I called her landlord, and asked him would he take a look for her in her apartment. He said, 'I have no key.' I said, 'You have no key? What do you mean you have no key? I never heard of a landlord who hasn't got a key!' I was getting excited, you see. I said, 'Please take a look in her window from the fire escape.' He did. He saw a light but couldn't see Sadye. I thought, Maybe she's lying on the floor and can't help herself. So I called 911, and they told me to call the 34th Precinct, where Sadye lives, and I did. Then I called Sadye again—and she answered. She just went out to shop and got talking to a neighbor at the market. I called the 34th Precinct back and said she just went to shop and was O.K. Sadye is a good girl. She is very intelligent, but, like all old-fashioned Jewish girls, she had little education and was kept in the home."

Gordon paid the check and said good night to Darr, and he and Jim walked the three blocks to the Vanguard. "Who's this Pat Metheny you have here tonight?" Jim asked when they reached the Vanguard door.

"I've been listening to his records off and on for two or three years, and at first I didn't like them," Gordon said. "It's taken me all that time to decide whether or not I wanted him in the place. Finally, he called me up, and I guess that helped me decide. He's just a kid, but he said he wanted to work at the Vanguard in the worst way. He said the Vanguard is where the vibes are—he used the word 'vibes.' He said the Vanguard was the place to be."

Gordon and Jim sat down at a table in the rear, and the music began. The band, which included Dewey Redman on tenor saxophone, Charlie Haden on bass, and Paul Motian on drums, started a fast blues. Metheny plays guitar. He uses a lot of amplifiers and sounds as if he were in Radio City Music Hall. Jim listened closely and looked over at Gordon. His arms were folded across his stomach, and his head was almost touching them.

"Max, you should be home in bed," Jim said, leaning over and touching one of Gordon's arms.

"What?" Gordon said, lifting his head. "I'm all right. I'm here. Metheny sounds pretty good. He sounds all right."

Two days later, Gordon's publisher gave an early-evening party at the Vanguard for Gordon's book. He paid for the booze and the music (a quintet led by the trumpeter Benny Bailey and including the tenor saxophonist Charlie Rouse), and the publisher supplied the food. A couple of hundred people came, and Gordon, circulating steadily, was invisible unless you were standing beside him. He was dressed in a stiff gray suit and a blue flannel shirt open at the neck. He said that this was the first time he'd worn the suit, even though he'd bought it four years before. John Wilcock, a founder of the *Village Voice*, said hello to him, and so did Stanton Wheeler, the Yale professor. Gordon said that Wheeler had taken him to the Yale Club bar, and that that was a sign of upward mobility. Jack Levine and his wife said hello. Gordon posed for a family photograph with Lorraine and their daughters. He had several glasses of champagne, which he doesn't like except at parties. During an intermission, Irwin Corey gave a speech from the bandstand, and called Gordon "a beacon." Betty Comden and Adolph Green said that their love for Gordon was "unbounded." The band returned, and Gordon, standing just in front, made Toscanini shushing gestures. Jim came up and put an arm around Gordon's shoulders. "Betty and Adolph almost made me cry, Jim," Gordon said. "What do you think of that?"

II

Barney Josephson, who is sixty-nine, still cherishes and grows eloquent over what he wrought at Café Society Downtown and Café Society

Uptown in the late thirties. His intent was simple and revolutionary: to present first-rate but generally unknown Negro and white talent to integrated audiences in honest, attractive surroundings. The performers at the clubs were as often as not discovered by Josephson or by the critic John Hammond, who provided the musical talent. Among the singers were Sarah Vaughan, Billie Holiday, Mildred Bailey, Lena Horne, Kenneth Spencer, Lucienne Boyer, Joe Turner, the Golden Gate Quartet, Patti Page, Josh White, Burl Ives, Big Bill Broonzy, Susan Reed, and Kay Starr. Among the comedians were Imogene Coca, Zero Mostel, Jimmy Savo, Jack Gilford, Jim Backus, Carol Channing, and Jim Copp. Among the dancers were the Kraft Sisters and Pearl Primus. And among the musicians were Frankie Newton, Red Allen, Bill Coleman, Teddy Wilson, Art Tatum, James P. Johnson, Albert Ammons, Meade Lux Lewis, Pete Johnson, Edmond Hall, Lester Young, Sidney Catlett, John Kirby, Eddie Heywood, Vincente Gomez, Django Reinhardt, Hazel Scott, Mary Lou Williams, Cliff Jackson, and Ellis Larkins. The surroundings in which this galaxy revolved were remarkable. Café Society Downtown in Sheridan Square was in a comfortable, L-shaped basement (capacity 210) decorated with funny murals by Adolf Dehn, Sam Berman, Ad Reinhardt, and Abe Birnbaum. The Uptown was on Fifty-eighth Street between Park and Lexington. It was an airy, two-story amphitheatre, with surrealistic murals by Anton Refregier. The bandstand was at the rear, and it was flanked by tiers of banquettes and tables that descended to a dance floor. A balcony with more tables ran along the back of the room. There were floor shows at both clubs at nine, twelve, and two, and a typical one at the Uptown included several numbers by Teddy Wilson's band (Joe Thomas, trumpet; Edmond Hall, clarinet; Benny Morton, trombone; John Williams, bass; Sidney Catlett, drums), one of them a flagwaver built around an invariably ingenious Catlett solo; half a dozen rushing, helter-skelter piano solos by Hazel Scott, who liked to jazz up Bach and "In a Country Garden"; Jimmy Savo's inimitable pantomime; and the loose-boned gospel songs and spirituals of the Golden Gate Quartet. In effect, three concerts, or recitals, were offered every night. Between the shows, which lasted about an hour, one ate and danced—not to an intermission trio but to Wilson's great band. Both clubs were congenial, clean, and pressureless. One could sit at the bar, nursing a single beer, for an entire evening. And parents actually *sent* their children to them unchaperoned for such state occasions as birthday parties and graduation parties. The food was fancier at the Uptown, partly because it brought in a different sort of trade and partly because of Josephson's mysterious belief that "people at Downtown just didn't pay much attention to eating, because they were in a basement." (Vide Max Gordon.) The service made both eighteen-year-olds and seventy-year-olds comfortable. "Many of the people who came to my clubs were like Eleanor Roosevelt," Josephson has said. "She had never been in a nightclub in her life, and she never went to another one."

Josephson, who has kept to himself since the Café Society days, has owned a Village restaurant called The Cookery for the past seventeen years. Located on the northeast corner of Eighth Street and University Place, it is a spic-and-span place furnished with plain, wood-topped tables and an omelette bar and decorated with Refregier hangings and murals. The prices are reasonable, and both cheeseburgers and steak all' pizzaiola are on the menu. The Cookery has never had music, but recently Josephson announced that the pianist Mary Lou Williams would soon open there. One afternoon, Josephson talked about his new venture, and about what he had been doing during the past twenty years. Josephson was sitting at a table in the Cookery with his wife, Gloria. She is intense, wiry, and fast-moving; Josephson is easy-going. He wears glasses, his cheeks are pink, his hair is white, and he looks like the late Ed Wynn. He speaks softly and quickly, has a high Wynn giggle, and is an effortless monologist.

Gloria Josephson departed, and Josephson began to talk. "I've had three other Cookerys uptown that were either unprofitable or were in buildings that were torn down. I live in the apartment house upstairs— right over the candy store, you could say, like the immigrants who roomed in the back of their shops and turned down the heat under their soup when the little bell out front rang and they had to go see who was in the store. I can't get over having Mary Lou Williams working for me again. She was at the Downtown for five years, and although she was never an overpowering attraction, she had a devoted coterie. Her coming back happened in the damnedest way. A young Jesuit named Peter O'Brien called me and said he had spent a lot of time recently with Mary Lou Williams, and could he come and see me? He did—in fact, he came several times—but he never mentioned just what he had on his mind. I found him a charming man, and if I were an important Catholic layman I'd tell the Pope to keep an eye on him. Then O'Brien appeared with Mary. I hadn't seen her for twenty years. From time to time she had called me, generally about someone she knew who was in trouble, but never about herself. Well, out it came: 'If I could only work for you again, Barney'—in that funny, chuckling way she has—'the happiest days of my life were at the Downtown.' She wasn't interested in cash, she said. She just wanted to work, and—well—she'd been getting seventeen hundred plus a week when she finally left me. I thought about it and looked into it and found I didn't need a cabaret license as long as there were no more than three instruments, all stringed. She brought along a bassist, Michael Fleming, and they opened soon after. I can't get over watching my old Cookery patrons watching her, and I can't get over how many of my Café Society customers have come in.

"The way I first got into the night-club business was far stranger. My parents came over from Latvia in 1900, and I was born two years later in Trenton. There were already two girls and three boys. My father was a cobbler and my mother a seamstress. When I was eight or nine months old my father stepped on a rusty nail and gangrene set in, and it was fatal. My mother was left with six children and no money. She went to work for a ladies' tailor, and an Irish lady who had twelve or thirteen children of her own took care of me during the day. My oldest brother, David, worked in a shoe store, and my oldest sister in a sweatshop, making ladies' silk bathrobes. We lived in an apartment so small one of my sisters slept in a closet. But my mother was a very frugal woman, and in time she had enough money to buy a house. It had four floors and cost a thousand dollars. It even had a bathroom, and the bathroom had a copper tub that David painted white every spring. When I got out of high school, David, who now had his own shoe business, told me that since we already had two brothers who were lawyers and I didn't look like medical material, I had better go into the shoe business with him. He had a keen sense of style. If he picked out a hundred pairs of shoes, they were *all* good. But he always overbought. He showed a profit—but in inventory, not cash. So along came the Depression, and there we were, with all those Whitehouse & Hardy shoes and $75,000 in accounts receivable. We went broke. My brother eventually started up again, but I didn't want any more of being an owner, so by the mid-thirties I was clerking in a shoe store in Atlantic City. I made forty dollars a month, lived in a four-dollar room, and ate my meals across the street in Bayliss's drugstore. But all this time I had the notion of starting a nightclub in the back of my head.

"When I worked for my brother, I used to go to the Marbridge Building on Herald Square, where all the shoe manufacturers showed their wares. I was an out-of-town buyer, so I was taken out to nightclubs. I liked what I saw, at least from a business point of view. A café restaurant has no inventory. The food turns over every day and the liquor once a week. And it's a cash business, or it was before credit cards and charge accounts. I had been to Europe in the early thirties and had visited the political cabarets, where there was very pointed satire. And I'd seen Gypsy Rose Lee doing a political strip tease at fund-raising affairs in New York for the Lincoln Brigade. I conceived the idea of presenting some sort of satire and alternating it with jazz music. But there was an even more important reason why I wanted to start a club. My fondness for jazz often took me to places like the Cotton Club in Harlem to hear Ethel Waters or Duke Ellington. Well, the Negro patrons were seated at the back in a segregated section—in a *Harlem* night club! And I'd been to the Kit-Kat Club in the East Fifties, which had all-black entertainment, plus black help, and yet not a Negro was admitted to the place. Until junior high I had gone to school with nothing but other Jews and the Irish. The first day I walked into class I saw a black boy sitting at a desk. The desk you picked became your desk for the year. Nobody had taken a desk near him, so I did, and we became great friends. And later I argued in a debate against military training in schools. I lost the debate, but afterward eight or ten boys got me in a corner and beat me up for what I'd said. So all those things were in my background, and New York in the mid-thirties echoed my feelings. It was the time of the labor organizers and the Ladies Garment Workers' show called *Pins and Needles* and the W.P.A. Art Movement and *The Cradle Will Rock*. I wanted a club where blacks and whites worked together behind the foot-lights and sat together out front. There wasn't, so far as I knew, a place like it in New York or in the country."

Two skinny, shy, dark-haired boys who turned out to be Josephson's sons, Edward and Louis, tumbled in the restaurant door and stopped at the table. They said they had taken the subway all the way from school on the upper West Side and hadn't got lost once. Josephson laughed. "Go and eat. Go and eat," he said. "Your mother's in the back.

"I made my decision early in 1938. I quit my job in Atlantic City and, with just $7.60 to my name, borrowed $6000 from two friends in Trenton. I had found a shuttered-up basement in Sheridan Square. The liquor license was $1200, the cabaret license $150, and the rent $200, and out the money began to go. And there was the decorating. I didn't want mirrors and draperies and velours. I wanted art. Sam Shaw, a painter and photographer, brought some of his W.P.A. Art friends in to do some murals—Adolf Dehn, William Gropper, Sam Berman, Gregor Duncan, and Abe Birnbaum. I paid them $200 each and gave them due bills of a like amount for food and liquor. Some of those due bills went on for years, too. I didn't tell them what to paint, only that the place would be called, in a tongue-in-cheek way, Café Society. Clare Boothe Luce had suggested it, through some mutual friends, and it fitted into my satirical scheme. A couple of girls on *Vogue* who had given me all sorts of ideas suggested we have a doorman but that he be dressed in a raggedy coat and white gloves with the fingertips out. They also suggested we find an Elsa Maxwell type who'd ride a scooter up and down the aisles. We did have the doorman for six or eight months, but we never found the right Elsa Maxwell. But the greatest help to me was John Hammond. He built my first band around the trumpet player Frankie Newton, and he brought in Albert Ammons and Meade Lux Lewis, the boogie-woogie pianists. And three weeks later he told me I had to have still another boogie-woogie pianist, Pete Johnson, but that Johnson only came with Joe Turner, the blues shouter. Jack Gilford was my first comedian. He'd been a stooge for Milton Berle at vaudeville houses like the Palace, where he was planted in the audience to shout insults at Berle onstage. John brought in the Golden Gate Quartet soon after, and they made the blood rush up my arms, which brought the goose pimples out when they sang—and here I was a disbeliever—'As they were driving the nails in His feet/You could hear the hammer ringing in Jerusalem's streets.' We opened on December 18, 1938. Village people came, and so did uptown types and the college kids. On Friday nights the place looked like Princeton, Yale, and Harvard rolled into one. It was a grand success, but I was losing money. I simply didn't know enough about this sort of merchandising. By the end of the first year I was $28,000 in the hole. It became a holding operation, paying out two hundred here and three hundred there to my creditors. I began to think that I had opened the club in the wrong part of town, that I should move uptown. I found a place on Fifty-eighth Street which had changed hands a lot and been burned out by some mugs trying to collect fire insurance. Ivan Black sent out a release saying that Café Society was so successful I was opening an uptown branch. Actually, I planned to dump the original club, but when people heard about the uptown club the crowd doubled downtown and I suddenly began making money. Café Society Uptown opened on October 8, 1940. A waiter I had stopped by to see me the other day, and he'd come across the menu for that night. It offered shrimps and oysters and clams, celery and olives, a couple of soups, a two-inch prime filet mignon with mushrooms, two vegetables, a choice of potatoes, and dessert. The price on the card was a dollar fifty! Uptown had cost me almost $30,000 to put in shape, all of it borrowed, but it started making money immediately, and by the end of that year I had paid off every cent."

The lights in the Cookery dimmed for the start of the dinner hour. Several groups of people came in, and Josephson excused himself to seat them. A headwaiter carried a huge poinsettia from the back of the restaurant and put it on one end of the omelette bar. Next to the bar was a brand-new grand piano. Josephson finished seating a family of five, then sat down. "That plant adds a little festivity to where Mary sits. She didn't want a Steinway, she wanted a Baldwin. I'm renting it, and if I decide to buy it the rent money goes toward the purchase." Josephson laughed. "I've got some accountant, and she's having fits over all this. 'You bring this piano player in here and it's doing nothing but costing money,' she says to me. 'Thirty dollars for that plant and nineteen dollars for the piano tuner each time he comes, and now he's coming *twice* a week. Next thing, you'll be out of business, with all your music.'

"I moved the Downtown show to the Uptown when it opened, and brought new people in Downtown. Mary took Hazel Scott's place, and Ida Cox came in for Billie Holiday. Teddy Wilson went Uptown and Eddie Heywood came in Downtown. In time I had a steady floating company of musicians and comedians and dancers and singers that moved back and forth between the clubs and that worked on a nearly permanent basis. It was a new concept in night clubs, and it gave the performers a sense of security most of them had never had before. It also gave them time to try out new routines and ideas. Hazel Scott was with me for seven years and the boogie-woogie boys, as we called them, for over four. Billie and Lena Horne stayed a year, and so did Jack Gilford. Jimmy Savo, who hadn't worked for ten years, stayed for three. People like Suzy Reed and Josh White were in and out for years, and so was Mildred Bailey. I don't know how I had this in me, but I learned how to shape talent, how to bring a performer's best out. I even costumed them, and I'd find myself in Bergdorf's with some cute new little singer and saying to one of those gray-haired salesladies, 'I'd like this young lady gowned.' Lena Horne was one of my first projects. She had worked in the line at the Cotton Club, and I first heard her, at John Hammond's suggestion, when she was singing with Charlie Barnet's band at the Paramount. She was beautiful, stunning, but it was hard to tell whether she could really sing or not. But I hired her, and at her first rehearsal I noticed that all her movements and routines were done in Latin rhythms, which were very big then. It didn't look right. I asked her if she was a Negro, and she bristled and said yes. I told her she could pass for anything, and she blew up. 'I don't dig you,' she said, and I said, 'Lena, there are dozens of nice Jewish girls from Brooklyn doing the Latin routines. Let me present you as a Negro talent. There won't be another like you for ten or fifteen years.' I got her singing blues and things like 'Summertime,' but she didn't have any contact with the audience because she wasn't putting feeling and meaning into what she sang. She would close her eyes when she sang or look at the ceiling. So I said to her, 'I know about white people and the Negroes and that most Negroes cannot look white people in the eye. Is that why you never look at your audience? Don't be afraid of them.' I sat at a ringside table, and when she looked at the ceiling I'd make signals. And I went over the lyrics of her songs, pointing out their meanings. Finally, she got to the point when she sang a blues of making people stand up and shout.

"Suzy Reed was the first Joan Baez—a beautiful girl with long reddish hair and a simple, direct manner. I made her keep her hair straight, told her not to wear makeup, and dressed her in little-girl frocks. At her first rehearsal she came out with a hop, skip, and jump and said, 'This is a zither.' I shouted, 'That's it, that's it! Don't ever change a thing!' And when she skipped out there in front of the audience and said, 'This is a zither,' she had them. I don't know whether it was because nobody had ever seen a zither before or whether it was the peaches-and-cream way she said it. I got Josh White to sit on a high stool when he sang, and I dressed him in open-necked shirts. He was a terror with the girls, and when they saw that neck—all muscles and tendons—they wanted to bite it. Of course, there were people I

missed and people I nearly missed. I missed out on Pearl Bailey alto-
gether. She struck me as a bit of a Tom, and I never hired her, but I
know now I was being over-sensitive. And I almost didn't get Pearl
Primus, a great dancer. She brought some records to her audition, but
she looked so awful I made an excuse about the phonograph being
broken and asked her to come back another time. She started to cry. I
excused myself and pretended to fuss over the phonograph. She put
on a record, took one fantastic leap, and that was it. John Martin of the
Times ranked her with Ted Shawn and Martha Graham. I had my
share of busts, generally with singers who, though I'd give them
months of vocal lessons, just couldn't sing. Sarah Vaughan didn't work
out, but for different reasons. I kept her six months, but people couldn't
understand her singing—all the strange twists and turns she did with
her voice—and she still didn't know how to get herself up right. Carol
Channing was a bust, too. She sang and did impersonations of society
dowagers and her special number was supposed to be a take-off of
Ethel Waters in *Cabin in the Sky*. It struck me the wrong way, and I
asked her not to use it. She felt I'd cut the heart out of her act, and she
went ahead and did it anyway, so I fired her. Jim Backus flopped. He
had another man with him, and I think they had a radio show, but
nobody listened to them at the club. I was beginning to learn that
although performers fail at one thing it doesn't mean they aren't good
at something else. So I was always very careful not to hurt people at
my auditions, especially because I never forgot a story Bernie Bernard
told me. He was a Hollywood agent who had booked vaudeville talent
in the Midwest. Two men auditioned for him, and he told them their
act wouldn't go. He looked at one of them and said, '*You* have some
possibilities, but your partner is impossible.' The next day the one he
had spoken to came back, very upset, and it turned out his partner had
just hung himself. When I was convinced a performer had gifts,

despite negative audience reactions, I stayed with him. Jack Gilford started slowly and he used to beg me to let him go, but I refused, and one night his time came. It was at the two o'clock show. Ammons and Johnson and Lewis and Billie Holiday were doing a benefit somewhere, and Joe Turner hadn't showed up, so all we had were the band and Gilford. He asked me what in God's name he was supposed to do. I told him he had to go on. The place was only half full, but a table of six or eight people had just come in. I'd been in enough places where the last show would be cancelled under such circumstances, but anyway Gilford, who was also the master of ceremonies, introduced the band, and they did their production numbers. Then he said, 'I would now like to introduce Albert Ammons, but Albert Ammons isn't here.' He got a laugh. Then he sat down at the piano and went into his beautiful pantomime with his great rubber face and made you *believe* he was Albert Ammons, by his motions and by scrunching up the back of his neck so that it looked like Ammon's rolls of fat. Then he did Meade Lux Lewis. Sometimes Lewis would start to fall asleep when he was playing, and I'd have to get someone to poke him, so Jack sat there nodding and swaying, and it was perfect. He did Billie and Johnson and Joe Turner and his own act, and the next day I had a call from one of the latecomers. It was Jed Harris, the David Merrick of the time, and he wanted Gilford for a revue called *Meet the People* that he was bringing to New York from California. Gilford joined it, and it was a great success. His Broadway career had begun. And do you know what he does every year on December 18, the anniversary of Downtown's opening? He sends me a telegram, wishing me well, and it doesn't matter where in the world he is.

"I also had a hand, in a roundabout way, in getting a girl named Betty Perske started. She was tall and thin and had a deep voice, and she used to hang around Downtown all the time by herself. I didn't care for single girls in the club, but I found out that she lived over on Barrow Street with her aunt, and I told my headwaiter to keep an eye on her. There was something special about her, and one night she told me she wanted to act. I said I'd arrange a meeting for her with Jack Shalitt, a talent scout for Howard Hughes. That was the last I saw of her. Time passed, and one evening Shalitt came in with a long face and asked me if I'd seen *Life* magazine that week. I had and I was delighted. There was a nine-page spread on Zero Mostel. I had hired Zero in the early days at the Downtown, when none of the uptown operators would touch him. Shalitt said, 'No, no, I don't mean that. I mean the girl on the cover. We didn't get her, we missed her.' I didn't recognize the girl or her name. Shalitt said she was Betty Perske. She *had* gone to Shalitt, and he'd sent pictures of her to Hughes. He wasn't impressed, and when Mrs. Howard Hawks saw them on his desk one evening at a dinner party and asked if she could show them to *her* Howard, Hughes said fine, and Hawks signed her and changed her name to Lauren Bacall."

It was eight o'clock, and Mary Lou Williams sat down at the piano. She was in a dark blue gown and her hair was parted on one side, débutante fashion. She looked around in a bemused way, rubbed her hands together, said something to her bassist, and started "My Blue Heaven." Her playing was sure and inventive and utterly relaxed. There was no microphone, but her long, graceful melodic lines moved easily through the room. "Yesterdays" went by, and it was followed by a rocking boogie-woogie number and a fast "Blue Skies." Josephson was smiling and his cheeks were flushed. "She's playing better now than she did thirty years ago," he said. The set ended; Mary Lou Williams greeted Josephson and sat down with Father Peter O'Brien, her admirer and protector.

"I got along very well with my performers, and they with me," Josephson said. "I always paid people at scale or better, and the highest salary I paid was thirty-five hundred a week. I also managed a lot of my performers for free when they went out to Hollywood and such. But no matter how well we got on, surprising things happened. I had an iron law at both clubs that there was to be no marijuana. When Billie Holiday was with me she'd get in a cab between shows and drive through Central Park, smoking. One night she came back and I could tell by her eyes that she was really high. She finished her first number and I guess she didn't like the way the audience reacted. Performers often wear just gowns and slippers, no underwear, and at the end of the song Billie turned her back to the audience, bent over, flipped up her gown, and walked off the floor." Josephson laughed. "I asked her backstage what in heaven's name she thought she was doing, and she just mumbled and slammed the dressing-room door.

"It had become the custom by the time Eddie Heywood came into the Downtown for the bandleader to double as emcee. Heywood stammered. He told me he was afraid people would laugh at him, and I told him not to worry. The first night was pretty bad, the next night better, and in a week there was only a trace. It must have had something to do with the intimacy of a microphone, and possibly also my confidence in him. Anyway, a couple of weeks later he explained that he was classified 4-F because of his stammering and that he was due for a medical review and could he quit emceeing for a few days until his stammer returned? He did, his 4-F status was renewed, and that night he announced shows again. One of the most surprising things also happened during the war, but it was at the Uptown. Jimmy Savo had a marvelous silent act in which he'd stop at a ringside table and pick up a customer's pack of cigarettes—this when cigarettes were so scarce. He'd take out a cigarette and, breaking it in two, light one half and put the other half in his pocket—all the while bowing and smiling to the owner of the cigarettes. Then he'd move to another table, still carrying the pack, and offer each of the people a cigarette, and keep this up until the cigarettes were gone. He'd return the empty pack to its owner, again bowing and scraping. He was in the middle of his act when a British sailor jumped up and grabbed a microphone and announced in a Cockney accent that he was going to sing a famous British Navy song about the time a British sailor floored 'that black nigger Jack Johnson.' Big Sid Catlett was sitting up there on the bandstand with his arms folded, and suddenly he picked up his drumsticks and began this tremendous thundering. The rest of the band joined in and the sailor was drowned out. The place was packed with servicemen, and they were outraged that one of them had been insulted, and there was nearly a riot. Afterward, I told the sailor that the word 'nigger' was not appreciated at Café Society Uptown, and he said he never knew there was anything insulting about the word and that he had black friends all over the world. It's a wonder more things didn't happen in those days. Like the time John Hammond and his wife came for dinner at the Uptown with Paul Robeson. Robeson and Mrs. Hammond danced. The headwaiter told me that the people at table forty-one would like to see me. There were two couples at the table, and one of the men said, 'Do you allow niggers to dance with white women in this place?' 'Sir,' I replied, 'we do not use that word in here. Furthermore, there is a law in this state against discrimination, and we abide by it. But it's still a democracy and you have a right not to like what you see.' 'Well, we don't like it at all,' he said. They walked out, but I made sure they paid their bill in full, even though they had just begun their shrimp cocktails.

"In the late forties, with both clubs going full steam, my life turned inside out. My brother Leon, who was working for me, was subpoenaed by the Un-American Activities Committee, which was headed by J. Parnell Thomas, the gent who later served time for misusing government funds. Leon was an avowed Communist and he refused to answer any questions, on the ground that the Committee was an illegal tribunal. He was cited for contempt, tried, and found guilty. His case was appealed to the Supreme Court, which refused to hear it, and he served ten months in prison. I think he may have been the first person to go to jail for contempt of the Committee. It was front-page stuff, and since no one knew who Leon Josephson was, he was always mentioned in the papers as the brother of Barney Josephson, the owner of Café Society Uptown and Café Society Downtown. The Hearst press — Pegler and Kilgallen and Lee Mortimer and Winchell — took off, and the innuendo, the guilt-by-association, began. Pegler devoted a column to Leon implying that he was a drug addict, and the last line was 'And there is much to be said about his brother Barney.' Just that, no more. So I was the brother of a Communist drug addict, I allowed Negroes in my clubs, I had introduced inflammatory songs like 'Strange Fruit' and 'The House I Live In,' and on and on. It ruined my clubs. Three weeks after the first uproar, business at the Uptown dropped 45 percent. I was determined not to give in to such viciousness, and I kept going for almost a year. But I had already lost $90,000, so I sold both clubs, and by 1950 I was out of the nightclub business and flat broke. I've only been into the Uptown once since it's become the Fine Arts Theatre, and that was to see *Rififi*. But all I could see were Teddy Wilson and Jimmy Savo.

"The reason I started a place like the Cookery was that I could be unknown, anonymous, and that's the way it's been. But this morning I ran into one of my old neighborhood customers, a lovely lady who has been eating here since we opened. She stopped me outside the supermarket and said, 'Mr. Josephson, you have made our world, our city a little bigger and a little better by bringing Mary Lou Williams into the Cookery, and I thank you.' That made me feel marvellous."

III

Part of the success of Bradley's, which occupies the ground floor of a brick-faced brownstone on University Place between Tenth and Eleventh Streets, is its benign mysteriousness, its avoidance of being categorized. "How can you get tired of a place when you don't know what it is?" one of its oldest customers has asked. "Every time you go in, you think you're going to find out. But you don't. So you go back again." Some of Bradley's customers think of it as a bar. They never get past the sixth or seventh bar stool (the bar is to the right of the door, and it runs about thirty feet), and can tell you little of the rest of the place. Some customers consider it a unique jazz club, where, seven nights a week from ten o'clock on, they can hear such pianists as Teddy Wilson, Tommy Flanagan, Hank Jones, and Joanne Brackeen. Other customers, particularly older locals, think of it as a restaurant where they can eat a peaceful early dinner and be home in time for the seven o'clock news. Still others, taking the food and the music largely for granted, consider it a semiprivate club, where on bleak evenings they can generally find a friend to talk to or, failing that, the proprietor himself, a quite famous Village person named Bradley Cunningham. Three of these club members recently talked about Bradley's. The first, a retired magazine editor, lives a block or two away. "Bradley's is a haven—figuratively and literally," he said. "One night, I beat two guys to the door who I'm sure were going to mug me. Bradley runs a clean house, a good house. The waitresses are friendly, the food is friendly, and there's always somebody to talk to. It attracts people who are not bores. I like the music—Tommy Flanagan best of all. The music just ripples off him. If anyone gets obstreperous in the place, God help him. The other evening, some guy who'd been drinking a lot brandished a gun, and Bradley threw him the length of the bar and into the street. He ran over him like a tank." The second club member is a feminist writer who lives in Murray Hill. "I'd never think of going to Elaine's by myself, but I've been in Bradley's alone many times," she said. "It's like a family there, a strange family—a family that can be a combination of writers and business types and musicians and neighborhood people, and even uptown people. Bradley runs a very good place. It's never been corny, and he doesn't tolerate silly business with drunks or people getting out of hand. He always keeps the place at an interesting level. Bradley first had a following when he tended bar at Chumley's, and when he moved to the 55 Bar people followed him. Then, when he opened Bradley's, they followed him there. He's attractive to both women and men, but he's hard to talk to and he's a hard person to know. He's very bright and he's very moral. If he cares about you, he's loyal to the death. He very rarely entertains at home. That's what Bradley's is for him—a living room to entertain his friends and himself in." The third club member is a painter who lives on Twenty-second Street. He likes to go to Bradley's and listen to the conversations at the bar: "One night, these two high-powered New York types were sitting there trying to one-up each other. One said, 'I went to camp with Bobby'—meaning Bobby Kennedy. The other said, 'Bobby and I were in the same class at Harvard.' The saxophonist Al Cohn was standing there, and he said, 'I met Babe Ruth once.' I asked Cohn what Ruth had said to him, and Cohn replied, 'Hiya, kid.' "

Bradley resembles a djinni. He is wide-shouldered, thick-chested, long-armed, rock-fisted, and tall, and he seems to swell as he talks to you. His head is covered with wavy, graying hair, and his eyes are green and deep-set. His face is craggy and handsome. He has a Kirk Douglas smile. He barely fits in his office, a tiny room off a passageway that runs from the dining room to the boxy, gleaming kitchen. The office has a small Formica-topped desk built into one wall, two desk chairs, a knee-high filing cabinet, and a narrow barred window with an air-conditioner in it. A big plastic container next to the window holds the waitresses' work shoes. A primping mirror hangs on the wall, and there are photographs of jazz musicians and singers. One day he sat in his office and talked. He had just had his lunch at the bar—two fried eggs over, bacon, and hashed-brown potatoes. He likes to talk, and he speaks in a universal, nondenominational drawl full of silences and stretched, see-through words. His laugh is robust and explosive. He lit a cigarette, and said: "Our menu hasn't changed essentially since we opened, thirteen years ago, so I've just hired my friend Miriam Ungerer, who writes about food and is married to Wilfrid Sheed. She's going to upgrade the menu—cue us in to the food explosion that's been going on out there. I've never been as interested in food as I should be. The first place I owned—the 55 Bar, at 55 Christopher Street—didn't have any at all. It was and is a drinking place that offers alcohol, cigarettes, and a jukebox. You'd have thought from the look of it that I threw a hand grenade inside and we were open. Actually, I put a billiard lamp over the table in the Hawaiian Room, which is a booth at the back of the place—the *only* booth—and I put Reynolds Wrap with holes punched in it over the other light fixtures. I replaced the twenty-eight-inch television set with a jukebox, because I didn't feel it would be consonant with the kind of place I had in mind to have neighborhood guys sitting around with a beer in hand watching *On the Waterfront*. In fact, I had a big list of people I didn't want in there. The people who worked for me weren't going to be subjected to the nonsense I'd been subjected to when I was a bartender. The 55 opened the night of the blackout in November of 1965, and we did a hundred and eighty-five dollars of business, which wasn't bad. The 55 eventually made a lot of money, and it could still be making money, but I haven't paid much attention to it in years. It got very raffish, even riffraffish. So I've sold it, and we're just waiting for the State Liquor Authority to O.K. the sale. When the 55 was on its feet, I began looking at a bar on University Place called the Stirrup. It was full of Naugahyde banquettes with aluminum trim, and the walls, which were varnished white pine, were covered with English hunting scenes. The place had a cheap blonde look. But there was something about it I liked very much, and in June of 1969 Jerry McGruddy and I took it over. We paid thirty-five thousand, and put fifteen more into it. McGruddy had been involved in Casey's, on West Tenth Street. Casey's was a beautiful jet-setty place, with good French food, that had been started by my friend K. C. Li. He was a Flying Tiger, and later he was in the tungsten business, and he had put a quarter of a million dollars into the restaurant. He and McGruddy parted company, and McGruddy was looking for something else. We replaced the banquettes with tables. We stripped the pine panelling, and stained it mahogany. It was my notion to put the mirror over the bar, and it was McGruddy's to call the place Bradley's. Everybody, including me, thought it was a bad idea, but I acquiesced as a consequence of my vanity, which is just below the surface." Bradley laughed, and went into the bar to get a Coke.

When he got back, he lit a cigarette. "We opened, and nothing happened. The help was getting paid, but we were scraping bottom. I used to stand out on the sidewalk and say to myself, 'There are eight million people in this city, and, please, all I need is forty of them.' The next spring, I went to Portugal for a couple of weeks to visit friends. David Sharpe, who had worked for me at the 55, had opened a place called Godot's, in Praia da Luz. I was in there talking to him one evening and I wasn't getting much response, and suddenly I realized why. He was doing exactly what I had been doing for months in New York—looking at the goddam front door and waiting for customers to walk in. Then my friend Danny Dod, who had come to Bradley's as bartender from the 55, called me in Portugal and told me I'd better get back—things were getting busy. *New York* had run a little piece with a photograph of Woody Allen and me at the bar. I came back, and we *were* busy, but the food wasn't together yet and we lost it. Then we hired Afortunado Perez as our chef. He's a Nuyorican, as the Puerto Ricans call people who emigrate to New York. He was the second cook at the Renaissance, on East Forty-ninth Street, and we offered him more money. He's been with us almost ten years, and he's hardworking and loyal. Then McGruddy suggested we hire a piano player. They'd had one at Casey's, and it had helped attract people. I play a little piano, so I put in an electric piano I'd bought from Roy Kral for $350, and the first person to play it was Dave Frishberg. Joe Zawinul, of Weather Report, came in later that year, and he started in full speed ahead—lighting a stick of incense and playing all this fast, heavy stuff during dinner. I told him none of this would do, and we had some words. But he settled down, and later we became pretty good friends. In fact, most of my friendships have started that way—clear the air first, then look around and see where you are. By 1972, the place had taken off. We were paying our bills, and even taking out a stipend. So McGruddy and I sat down and talked over a buy-out arrangement, which would give each partner first chance to buy out the other for an agreed-upon sum of money. We discussed the amount, and it all drifted off and we never put anything on paper. Then John Kadesch, a bartender and my day manager, and Timothy Duffy, who had worked for me and was a bartender at the Buffalo Roadhouse, told me that McGruddy was talking about selling them his share of the business. McGruddy wasn't satisfied with the price we had discussed, and they were willing to pay him more. I suggested to Kadesch and Duffy that I was shocked by the news. I told McGruddy that I was disappointed in him. I stared at the wall for a while. I saw a couple of lawyers who didn't have any ideas;

then someone put me onto a restaurant lawyer that Elaine Kaufman had used. Kadesch and Duffy gave McGruddy a thousand dollars down, and he took off. They started behaving like partners—ordering drinks on the house, and such. I told them they had absolutely no say in anything, because they were not on the board of directors and couldn't be unless they were voted on by me. There was a Mexican standoff, which I watched with a certain relish. They sued me in State Supreme Court. The case became bogged down in technicalities, and the stock reverted to McGruddy. He came in for lunch, and I told *him* he no longer had any say in the business. He sued me in District Court, and we settled out of court, and I bought his stock. My landlady had put the building Bradley's is in on the market, and other wolves were gathering. With my sister's help, I bought the building, and now we're as safe as a church."

Bradley said goodbye to his day cook, to his waitresses, and to Tommy Derecas, his manager. He walked to his apartment, where he lives with his wife, Wendy, and their son, Jed. The apartment is on the south side of Sheridan Square. Once or twice a block, he greeted someone he knew. On the way, he talked about his new sobriety. 'I started drinking heavily in California after the Second World War. I was depressed. I read Proust for a week or two instead of looking for work, which I hate to do. Drinking can get to be a debilitating hobby. It can get to be a full-time job, which is what it was by the time I finally quit. I was drinking around the clock. I'd hang out at Bradley's all night with the piano players, and I'd sleep off and on all day. I thought I was having the time of my life, but I wasn't going anywhere. I was on the roller coaster, and I was bored with it. I knew I was bored, but couldn't seem to get off. I was never one of those drinkers who carom off the wall. I'd be smashed and no one would know it. I had also gotten enormous. I had outgrown

Brooks Brothers and had to buy my clothes at the baby-elephant shop. My son Jed, who's six, told a schoolmate, 'My father is older than your father, and he's as big as a refrigerator.' In November of 1981, I went to St. Mary's Rehab, in Minneapolis. They search your luggage for pills or whatever, and put you on Librium the first few days. You are assigned to a group, which meets twice a day, and it's no holds barred. You also have three lectures a day, and you have to write a paper on why you are there, what kind of person you are. Most people write pretty bland things. I tried to be as tough as I could on myself, but it wasn't easy. The next thing was Family Week. A member of your family visits, and there is a brutal confrontation in which you give your version of your drinking and the family member gives his. There were some pretty red faces. I got back here just before Christmas. It's a very gradual thing. They told me I wouldn't be completely right for five years. I'm still not doing too well at filling up my life. I may go to Bradley's once or twice a day, but the Greek, as Tommy Derecas calls himself, is a workaholic. I leased a Saab Turbo, and I'll run down to the Bowery to buy some bar stools, or somewhere else to pick up candleholders. Nice days, I drive up to the Palisades to hit golf balls. Every Monday evening, I go to my FACT meeting. That's the Family Alcoholism Consultants Team. It's a structured professional therapy group, and we talk about the past week and what might come."

Bradley lives in a loft about the same size as Bradley's. At its east end are a bedroom, a bathroom, and a walk-in closet that serves as a dressing room. The main room, which is two stories high and has a balcony on one side, starts with a galley kitchen and dining area, moves past the front door and an upright piano (once at Bradley's), encloses a living area that includes a couple of desks (one is Jed's), an Eames chair that belonged to Paul Desmond, a television set, and some sofas and chairs, and ends at Roy Kral's electric piano and the door to Jed's room, which looks like F. A. O. Schwarz. The loft has a concrete floor, part of it painted beige and part of it covered with a biege carpet. The walls are off-white. The room is lined with windows, and flights of pigeons comb past them into the low sky. Bradley likes nothing better than strolling from his bedroom to the electric piano and back, a round trip he estimates at 180 feet. "I love this apartment, and I love New York City," he said. "I can look up Seventh Avenue from my windows. I can look out into Christopher Park. I can look down West Fourth Street and Grove Street and Christopher Street. One Thanksgiving evening, Wendy called me to the window, and the traffic was backed way up Seventh Avenue—people trying to get to the Holland Tunnel, or, as Wendy aptly put it, 'Underneath the river and through the ghetto to Grandmother's house we go.' I can look out and everybody is carrying on busy as hell, and I can hear that murmur, that undercurrent, that goes on all the time in New York. New York is *power*, yet at the center of that power is a certain amount of calm. When I step outside, I love to see the red lights turn green, especially in the rain. And when Con Edison is digging, and they put up all those lights, it knocks me out. You can do what you want in New York. You can start a business and people will let you live. In a small town, if they don't like you they'll figure a way to keep you out. In New York, you take people one by one. You learn what the city is when you come back after a vacation. It's a shock. You have to tighten your reflexes, tighten your act. You have to regalvanize yourself into the city's tempo. You've got to rally, as one of my bartenders used to say."

Bradley sat down abruptly at the upright piano by the door and went into Thelonious Monk's "Crepuscule with Nellie," following it with Monk's "Ruby, My Dear." He has been playing the piano since he was a teen-ager, and he is a good modern chordal pianist. He has had countless impromptu early-morning lessons from the likes of Jimmy

Rowles and Cedar Walton. While he played, he shouted, "I guess I'm glad I'm not an itinerant piano player, but it sure would be a fine way to travel to Japan and Europe and Australia!" He started "Shall We Dance?" and sang it in a pleasant light baritone. Before he finished, the telephone rang, and it was his sister Nancy, calling from California. He talked four or five minutes, hung up, and poured himself a glass of iced tea.

"I was born four years after Nancy, on September 9, 1925, in Chicago, which I left almost immediately, and didn't get back to until last December, when I was on my way home from St. Mary's Rehab. My mother was Gretchen Dau, and she was from Galveston, Texas. She was born in 1890, and had three younger sisters and a younger brother. Their father, Fred Dau, was a clipper-ship captain from Hamburg. He was a good old guy who lived to be eighty-eight. We called him Opa, and Grandma Oma. My mother was a charming chick. She had blue eyes and blond hair, and tended to be a little over-weight. She didn't drink and she didn't smoke, and she had a good sense of humor. She had a very strong sense of justice, and the vocab-ulary to go with it. She was never obscene, but there were always a lot of 'bastards' and 'sons of bitches' flying around. She liked men, and men liked her, because she could talk about anything. She married my father, Charles Bradley Cunningham, in 1919, and they were divorced when I was still a little kid. He was from Buffalo, and was a pilot in the First World War. He never got overseas. He was in the insurance busi-ness, but he had a tendency to become involved in things like selling subterranean real estate in Florida. I think Gretchen divested herself of him when he got the notion of taking arms down to Central America in a yacht he had bought and bringing back rum, it being Prohibition time. Anyway, there was a shipwreck that threw everything into a different motion. The last time I saw him, I was six or seven. We lived in Altadena, California—2756 Highland Avenue—and my father had a Studebaker convertible with about thirty-eight cylinders. It was tan, with green pinstripes, and it made this huge *vroom vroom vroom* when he stepped on the gas. One day, he took me to the Annandale Golf Club, and we had a terrific time. At the end of the afternoon, he told me he was leaving us. That broke me up so much that I wasn't able to talk about it without weeping until six months ago. He wrote me a couple of times during the war, telling me to be tough, and he died not long after. Many years later, I asked my Aunt Helen Pritchard—one of my mother's sisters—what he was like, and she surprised me. Here was this seventy-five-year-old lady with concrete-gray hair, and she said, 'I was the first to go out with him, and through me he met Gretchen, and that bitch—he never had eyes for anyone else.' She died the winter before last, in her eighties, in Killeen, Texas.

"When I was two and a half or three and Nancy was seven, we were put in the Bon Avon School, in San Antonio, Texas. After a year or so, we joined Gretchen in New York. She was always in government or politics. At the time, she was a friend of John Raskob, who was chairman of the Democratic National Committee. Later, she was in charge of the women's part of the D.N.C., and she was a director of the League of Women Voters for four or five years. She was also a member of the woman-suffrage movement. But I don't think she ever had the power she felt she deserved. We lived at the Ritz-Carlton, at Madison Avenue and Forty-sixth Street. I remember shrimp cocktail served in blue cut glass, and throwing snowballs down on the people on Madison Avenue, and riding a tricycle up and down the corridors. I remember being taken to Central Park by a wonderful Irish cat named Alan. He was the chauffeur of a friend of my mother's. I also remember going with a Mrs. Finnegan, whom we hated. We called her Mrs. Vinegar. I went to a nursery school, and the apartment was always full of people like Hiram Johnson, a senator from California, and Claude Bowers, who was the Ambassador to Spain, and William McAdoo, another senator from California, and Rabbi Stephen Wise, an early Zionist. Then we moved to Altadena. We were in the foothills of the San Gabriel Mountains, just below the Mt. Wilson Observatory, which had the world's largest telescope before the Mt. Palomar mirror was ground. Roosevelt came to power, and Gretchen went to Washington to work in the N.R.A. Aunt Helen came, with her daughter Jacquelyn, to take care of Nancy and me. I was put in the Trailfinder's School, which was run by an early conservationist named Harry James. It was strictly male, and everyone wore a uniform—corduroy shorts or knickers. I was terribly unhappy. You know—deserted again. There was a Hopi chief's son in the school, and one day when I was feeling low he said, 'Hey, Brad, you feel bad?' Sympathy, I thought, but all he wanted was to divert my attention while somebody else held a magnifying glass up to my neck in the sunlight. One summer, I went to Yosemite with some wilderness-prone people from across the street named Adams. Another summer, I visited Daus in Galveston and Houston. Oma would say, 'If you don't behave, I won't give you the *kruste*,' which means 'bread crust.' It was the only hangover from the German days I ever saw in my family. My mother materialized for a summer and rented the Sunset Hotel in Laguna Beach with two or three other people. Laguna was beautiful then. It was like the Mediterranean—nothing but white stucco walls and red tile roofs. I went to a public school in Pasadena, and on to Eliot Junior High, in Altadena, where I began to get in trouble. I'd skip school and hitch to Santa Anita. They put me in a private school near Caltech, and I got in a fight and was asked to leave. I went to the Cathedral High School, a Catholic school, in Los Angeles, where I lasted two or three months. It was full of Mexican and Irish kids, and was the toughest school I was ever in. After that, I was put in the Bonita Vista High School, in Chula Vista, on the way to San Diego. I left there in the ninth grade—this would be around 1940—and joined my mother in Needham, Massachusetts. She had just remarried. My stepfather was from San Francisco, and his name was Frederick William Witt. He worked in the Treasury Department. They were married at the Ritz-Carlton in Boston. I went to a school in Wellesley, then to one in Providence. Then my folks moved to Washington, D.C., to a nice pad at Thirty-first and R, near Dumbarton Oaks, and I was asked to go along. I went to Western High, and didn't do too well at my studies. What happened was I went to bed one night five feet nine inches and woke up six feet two, and when the basketball coach said to me in September 'Cunningham, are you coming out for basketball?' I was puffing and told him 'No, I don't have the energy'—which was true. I just sat around and played Benny Goodman records and was clumsy. I was passing a sugar bowl when I was introduced to some senator and I stood up and dropped it and shook hands with him. I finished my preparatory-school career at Millard Prep, on Connecticut Avenue. It was a mill full of Army brats prepping for West Point. I took the West Point exam and did surprisingly well in English and history but not too well in math. So I went to Haverford College, and loved it. I played left tackle on the football team. By this time, it was 1943, and I was about to get drafted. Because I didn't want to get lost in the Army, I enlisted in the Marines, and by December of that year I was at Parris Island."

Wendy and Jed came in, home from school. They are vigorous and attractive. Wendy has long brown hair, sharp wide-set hazel eyes, and a good smile. Her shoulders are broad, and her waist is trim. She has a big, direct way of talking. Jed, as tall as an Indian club, is her spit and image. His hair is light, and he was wearing a Yankee jacket, a blue

button-down shirt, a navy-blue-and-red clip-on tie, and navy-blue corduroy pants. His eyes are as wide apart as Wendy's. Bradley nodded at
everyone and sat down at the electric piano and played "Easy Living."
Jed washed his hands and got his Sonic Fazer from his room and
zapped Bradley from behind a sofa. Bradley played on. Wendy gave Jed
a glass of milk and some Fig Newtons. Jed brandished a wooden
American flag he had made in wood-working class, and sat down. He
took a half-moon bite out of a Fig Newton and drank his milk. Then he
got out his snow walker—an eighteen-inch-high replica of the towering war machines that walk across the opening sequences of *The
Empire Strikes Back*. He made the snow walker go half the length of the
room, and it moved, and even looked, like Bradley. Jed climbed the ladder that leads to the balcony in the living room, and rescued a ball that
he had kicked up there last night. Bradley announced that he was
going out to buy some Coke and the *Village Voice*.

Wendy sat down at the kitchen table and lit a cigarette. "Bradley's a
lovable bully," she said. "He's a manipulative man. He used to edit my
grammar when we were arguing. He's got excessive charm when he
wants something. He's witty. He'll flirt his way out of things. He's kind
to people he respects, but he can be terribly critical of people—
particularly women. He can't cope with certain things—death, for
one. If someone he's fond of is ill and dying, he'll just shut it out. He'll
cop out. We have respect for each other's intelligence. I'm not as well
read as he is, and I never will be, but he learns as much from me as I
learn from him. Bradley demands a good deal. There's a lot of cacoph-
ony and eighth notes and blaring colors when he's around. He's at the
piano, he's on the telephone, he has both TV sets going. He travels
with noise. I met him at Bradley's when I went to work there as a waitress, a month after the place opened. I'd just come off a bad short marriage. I come from Cochituate, about fifteen miles west of Boston,

where I was born, in 1946. My parents live in Florida now, but they were hardworking folks. My father was a house painter, and my mother did secretarial work. I went to a two-year college in Illinois. Then I came to New York. I was Wendy the waitress at Bradley's for three years. Then Bradley fired me, and I moved in with him. We were married in December of 1975, at St. Luke in the Fields. Jackie Cain and Roy Kral were the witnesses, and Alec Wilder gave me away. Jed was born in 1976. This place was a mess when I moved in. I've scraped and sanded and repainted. I've built a big storage space behind Jed's room which Bradley calls 'the garage.' It's what I do best. Things have improved considerably since Bradley quit drinking. I used to feel like a single woman with a kid and a tenant who paid a very good rent. I finally gave him an ultimatum—quit or Jed and I leave—and that is what got him off to St. Mary's Rehab."

Bradley returned, riffled through the *Voice* and said that he was going to run up to the 9 W Golf Range and hit a couple of buckets of balls. He got his Saab out of a garage a block or two away and drove up Twelfth Avenue to the Fifties, where he turned onto the West Side Highway. He is a careful, vociferous driver, and he opened up on the drive. The Marines were still on his mind. "After boot camp, I went to combat-intelligence school at Camp Lejeune. Then it was through the Panama Canal to Hawaii to the Eighth Marines on Tinian Island. We landed the day after the invasion. I was a scout who shuttled back and forth between headquarters and frontline observation posts. Just before the island was secured, I watched the Japanese soldiers throw themselves off the cliffs into the sea. I was asked if I wanted to go to Japanese-language school, and I said yes. It was eight hours a day for ten weeks on Saipan. We learned conversational Japanese and also some *kanji*, which is ideographic writing, and *katakana*, which is phonetic spelling. In April of 1945, we landed on Okinawa; then we were assigned to the floating reserves on a troop ship in the South China Sea. One day, the Red Cross or somebody dumped a whole bunch of books down on us jarheads from a higher deck, and the only one left after the scramble was a fat volume of Mr. Leo Tolstoy named *War and Peace*, which is how I got acquainted with him. We went back to Okinawa after the Battle of Naha, and my job was to talk Japanese soldiers out of the bunkers and caves they were holed up in and interrogate them. A lot of them were simply shot by the Americans, but when we did get to question a prisoner he'd generally tell us everything. Captured G.I.s were only supposed to give their name, rank, and serial number, but the Japanese had never been told anything similar, because they were never expected to be captured. My great contribution to the war was questioning an officer and finding out about a huge cave filled with snipers—several hundred of them. Finding out about that cave saved a lot of lives, and I'm proud of that. When Okinawa was secured, we went back to Saipan to get ready for the landing on Japan itself. Then they dropped the bomb, and the war ended. We landed at Nagasaki, and it was just as devastating as everybody said. We eventually moved to Misumi, thirty-five miles away, and they sent all the confiscated weapons to us and we dumped them offshore in the Ryukyu Trench, which is about twenty thousand feet deep. I stayed in Japan until February of 1946, when I had enough points to come home. I loved Japan and I liked the Japanese. By the time I left, I could speak fairly well, but I still had trouble understanding when I was spoken to. So what I would do was construct these elaborate and complicated sentences that would require only a yes-or-no answer."

Bradley swept across the George Washington Bridge and onto the Palisades Interstate Parkway. The Hudson was afternoon gray, and the sun hit Bradley right in the eyes until he turned onto the parkway, where it dodged through the trees on his left. "I went back to Haverford, but after a term or two I got antsy and asked for a leave of absence. My mother was living in Georgetown, and she told me I couldn't sit around there. I went to Coral Gables, Florida, where I had a cousin. I drove a truck in Miami, and met a girl there, and we got married—in the summer of 1947. She was a student at the University of Miami. Then I enrolled in the School of Foreign Service at Georgetown University, and we moved to Washington. She worked as a secretary, and I worked part time in the House mailroom—and we split. I did a year or so at the foreign-service school, and took off for California, where my sister Nancy was. I lived in Laguna Beach, which was as beautiful as ever. I'd work like a son of a bitch as a carpenter all day at three dollars an hour and drink all night. One night, this guy who worked at the Sandpiper, where I hung out, said, 'Why don't you work behind the stick?'—which means tend bar. 'You can go to the beach by day and make money by night.' So I did. I moved over to a really neat placed called Christian's Hut. It had Hawaiian music and Polynesian décor, and the help wore Hawaiian shirts. It was part of a chain that had been started by a brother of the cameraman on *Mutiny on the Bounty*. The Pitcairn Island sequences had been filmed on Catalina Island, and when the picture was finished this brother bought the set and opened the first Christian's Hut in it. A girl named Jean Packard came in to play piano. She was a good pianist with a great sense of inner harmonies. We got married in Tijuana after a bullfight. Then I decided to come to New York. It was 1956. I had worked behind the stick at the Brussels and the White House Café in Laguna Beach. I was a good bartender, but I was a little ashamed of the work. So I landed a job at Grey Advertising producing radio commercials, but by the time I knew what I was doing they had fired me. I ended up behind the stick at Nob Hill, at Forty-fourth and Second. Then I went to Stefan's, on Christopher Street. George Darcy owned Nob Hill, and he gave me a reference that went like this: 'He has a good appearance, he's a good bartender, it's beneath him to steal, and he's never lost a fight.' I have a reputation for being tough, but I'm not a tough guy. I don't have a taste for it. Situations come up that simply have to be taken care of, like the wrong people coming into Bradley's when you've asked them to stay away. Ray Santini bought Chumley's, on Barrow Street. It had been an old newspaperman's hangout. I worked behind the stick, and I managed the place. It was a beautiful little dugout bar. I was there a couple of years. After the No Name Bar and the Corner Bistro, I opened the 55. Jean and I split while I was at the No Name. But what does it all matter? Every once in a while, Wendy's parents ask her, 'When is Bradley going to get a job?' "

Goodbye Oompah

HARVEY PHILLIPS

In the early eighteen-forties, Hector Berlioz made an exploratory musical tour of Germany, and in one of the exhaustive letters he sent back to France he said, "The bass tuba . . . has completely dislodged the ophicleide in Prussia. . . . [It] is a large brass instrument . . . fitted with a mechanism of five rotary valves which gives it an enormous range in the lower register. The lowest notes of all are a little blurred, it is true; but when doubled an octave higher by another bass tuba, they take on amazing richness and resonance; and in the middle and upper registers the tone is impressively noble, not at all flat like the ophicleide's but full and vibrant and well matched with the timbre of trombones and trumpets, to which it serves as a true bass, blending perfectly with them." For all of Berlioz's perspicacity, about the only thing that happened to the tuba during the next hundred years was its absorption into the symphony orchestra and the marching band. Then, twenty years ago, Ralph Vaughan Williams wrote his pioneering Concerto for Bass Tuba and Orchestra, which was followed by Paul Hindemith's Sonata for Tuba and Piano. Before that, tubists had eased their urge to solo by playing transcriptions of Bach and Beethoven and by transposing solo pieces that had been written for other instruments.

Vaughan Williams and Hindemith broke a vicious circle: no one had written pieces for solo tuba because there were none to point the way, none to suggest the marvellous tonal and lyrical possibilities of the instrument, and there were none to point the way because—and so forth. In the fifties and sixties, post-Vaughan Williams–Hindemith, a further trickle of tuba compositions appeared, many of them written by Alec Wilder, and in the seventies this freshet suddenly became a river. There are now almost four hundred solo compositions for tuba—for tuba and piano, for tuba and string quartet, for tuba and nine French horns, for tuba and horn and piano, for tuba and woodwind quintet, for tuba and four horns and percussion, for tuba and small orchestra—as well as tuba octets, quartets, trios, duos, and solos.

The ongoing elevation of the tuba from the laughingstock of musical instruments to one of its kings is mainly the doing of Harvey Phillips, a tubist and a professor of music at Indiana University, who has spent over half his life in the service of his instrument, which he plays better than anyone else in the world. (Tubists are multiplying in direct ratio to their repertory; there are now nearly a thousand members of TUBA—the Tubists Universal Brotherhood Association, an organization Phillips helped get on its feet.) Many of his colleagues rank him the finest living brass player and, by extension, one of the certified virtuosos of his time. But Phillips is not interested in pecking orders, real or imagined. His passions are the betterment of the tuba, the betterment of those who play it, and the betterment of American music. "It's a time of marvels in wind playing," James T. Maher, the omnifarious writer and a close observer of Phillips, has said. "There have been and are an extraordinary number of good players, like Julius Baker on flute and Reginald Kell on clarinet and Bernard Garfield on bassoon and Leon Goossens on oboe. And horn players like the late

Dennis Brain and the late John Barrows. Harvey Phillips certainly belongs in that company. He also belongs to the American school of wind playing. The English school—Brain, Kell, and the like—has its elegance, its sense of *ensemble*; the American school has more sinew, even a little roughness. The players in the American school take incredible chances, despite the terrific problems wind instruments inherently have. Harvey has uncanny phrasing—which is not the right word. It makes him sound too technical. What he does is point up the poetry in what he plays. And he is apt to play anything, since there is really no longer a sharp division between jazz wind players and classical wind players and the like. Wind players now move in a great gray area, in which the best are apt to play a different kind of music every day of the week. It doesn't matter if it's a TV commercial or a recital or a jazz date or movie music, but it does matter how well they execute. Harvey wants to be the best tubist there is, and he wants to shape a new world of sensibility in all music. He's willing to tackle every side of the problem. He keeps a pleasant demeanor, but he's tough and he's obsessive. Along with all the order he professes to exhibit in his comings and goings, he likes a bit of daily chaos. Then he has something on which to demonstrate his ability to impose order."

Phillips is over six feet and of considerable girth. His fingers are sausages and his feet gunboats. He has a long, full face and wavy black hair, and he wears glasses. His cherubic lips bear the pinkish aureole that is the unmistakable badge of the professional brass player. He has an old-fashioned, almost goody-goody look. But his deep-set eyes are savvy and laughing, and his generally placid expression conceals a mischievous intelligence. Phillips is celebrated for his outsize ways, for his studied chaos, but his excesses—harmless except when the exhaustion they lead to topples him and he goes down like a sequoia—are positive and even altruistic. Here are half a dozen instances of his Paul Bunyan ways:

When he was on the road in Kansas, 1960, with the New York Brass Quintet, he suggested that the group spend a night with one of his sisters, who lived on a farm handy to their next concert. He drove the unwitting musicians twenty miles out of the way to an abandoned farm he knew of. There he went through an extended routine of calling his sister through the gaping front door of the farmhouse and then, scratching his head, hallooing into the swaying barn, all the while furtively studying the frozen expressions on his colleagues' city-slicker faces.

In 1962, he carted enough hickory wood from the Midwest to the Aspen Music Festival to smoke twenty-eight sides of pork, twenty hams, and twelve trout. He also transplanted enough mint to furnish several hundred mint juleps. And when the Festival officials refused to specially honor Gunther Schuller, who was coming to the Festival and is one of his heroes, he hired an Aspen restaurant and threw a party himself.

Phillips always needs money for tuba-uplift events. He has recently financed four—the First International Tuba Symposium-Workshop, held in the spring of 1973 at Indiana University and attended by four hundred interested composers, professional tubists, and students, and three Octubafests, the first of which was held at Indiana in the fall of 1973 and was attended by many of his students and former students. Whenever Phillips says "Octubafest," a "good pun!" light goes on in his eyes. And it goes on when he talks of his most recent tuba-uplift idea—a toothpaste called Tuba.

During the past twenty-five years, Phillips has played with or been a member of the New York Philharmonic, the Metropolitan Opera Orchestra, the New York City Ballet Orchestra, the Ringling Brothers and Barnum & Bailey Circus Band, the Sauter-Finegan orchestra, the NBC Opera orchestra, the United States Army Field Band, the *Bell Telephone Hour* orchestra, the New York Brass Quintet, the Symphony of the Air, the Goldman Band, the *Voice of Firestone* orchestra, and Orchestra U.S.A. The result is an inveterate traveler who cannot stand being late or missing engagements. He once started out from New York for a one-night stand in Springfield, Massachusetts, on a train to Scarsdale, where an oboist he had just met was to pick him up and drive him the rest of the way. But he fell asleep on the train and woke up at the end of the run, in White Plains. He couldn't remember the oboist's name or phone number, so he hailed a White Plains cab and took off for Springfield. The tab was seventy-five dollars, but he walked onstage just ahead of the conductor.

While he was assistant to the president of the New England Conservatory of Music, in Boston, he kept his chair in the New York City Ballet Orchestra. During the season, he'd finish a full day's work in Boston and take the six-thirty flight to New York, arriving at eight-fifteen at Lincoln Center; then he'd catch the last flight back. Once in a while, he'd fly to New York in the morning for a recording session, fly back for an afternoon meeting at the Conservatory, take an evening shuttle for his New York Ballet performance, and be home in bed in his Boston suburb by one-thirty. During this period, his practicing often fell into arrears. He recalls getting back to Boston early one morning and finding his wife, Carol, and their three children (Jesse, Harvey, and Thomas) asleep spoon-fashion in bed together. Phillips is as passionate about his family as he is about the tuba. Knowing that he had to practice but wishing to be with them, he turned on a light, sat down with his tuba, and played until dawn. It was a perfect session: nobody woke up, and he proved to himself again that when it is properly played the tuba is the softest instrument in the world.

Phillips refuses to be separated from his family for any length of time. He and Carol went everywhere together during the childless years of their marriage, and after he was injured in an automobile collision in New York she carried his tuba to every gig for six months. Nowadays, when an engagement keeps him away for more than five days Carol and the children join him, no matter the time of year. On the way home, Carol drives and he sits in the back and practices.

In 1974, Phillips decided that New York was ready for the tuba, and he organized two extraordinary events. The first was a concert of Christmas carols in Rockefeller Plaza, in front of the big tree, by 250 tubists who had come, at Phillips's invitation, from all over the country at their own expense. A couple of dozen carols had been freshly scored by Alec Wilder in four- and six-part harmony, and the massed sounds were unique and stirring and noble—so much so that the concert, by 400 tubists, will be repeated every year. (The music at the 1974 rehearsal, held in a long, low, steaming corridor on the second floor of the RCA Building, was, by virtue of being compressed and yet augmented by the milieu, even more spectacular. Phillips, in his shirt-sleeves, closed the rehearsal by shouting to his tubists, "*Now* let them talk about their oompahs!") His second New York event took place early in January of 1975. He rented Carnegie Recital Hall for four evenings and an afternoon, and gave five marathon tuba recitals, during which he played thirty-nine pieces. He was abetted by a small jazz group, the New England Conservatory Chamber Orchestra (shipped south at his expense), a string quartet, a woodwind quintet, several pianists, a host of horn players, two percussionists, and three tubists. There were jazz numbers arranged by Dick Cary and Johnny Carisi; lyrical serenades and sonatas by Alec Wilder; the Hindemith and Vaughan Williams pieces; David Baker's jarring, complex exercise for tuba and string quartet; Bernhard Heiden's brand-new piece for tuba and nine horns;

a short, pastel composition by Eddie Sauter; Richard Peaslee's spooky, melodramatic "The Devil's Herald," its ink barely dry, for tuba, four horns, and percussion; and Gunther Schuller's Capriccio for Tuba and Small Orchestra. During the eleven days the recitals involved, Phillips rehearsed sixty-six hours, and on two days he did his old New York-Boston-New York shuttle act. Not only did his lip survive seventy-six hours of playing, but immediately after the final concert he went to the Roosevelt Hotel, where he performed the Baker tuba-and-string-quartet piece again for a conference of brass men. The next day, he drove Carol and the children through a blizzard to Boston to record Schuller's Capriccio. And the day after, he recorded the Vaughan Williams Concerto.

Phillips started rehearsing in New York a month or so before the recitals. The rehearsals were held in half a dozen of the plethora of studios scattered about the city. He went to two or three or four a day, and most lasted three hours. To relax, he talked a good deal during the cab rides between studios. He keeps his eyes closed when he talks at length, as if he were watching his words on a screen inside his head, and he speaks in a deliberate, quietly swinging way.

"The origins of the tuba are not at all clear. But I do know that it followed the ophicleide, which followed the serpent. I also know it became possible through the invention of valves. The serpent was made of wood and leather, and it had finger holes. It looked like an S with a big curlicue at either end, and I think it appeared around 1600. The ophicleide was invented in 1817 by one Jean Hilaire Asté, and it was a tall, thin tuba, a kind of spinster tuba. Not long after Berlioz made his German discovery, the ingenious Adolphe Sax was at work in Paris making tubas. Eventually they came in many shapes: some bells pointed up, some pointed backward, some were like tear-drops. One model straddled both shoulders. But eventually Sax determined pretty much what we now know as their shape—valves and all. The tuba inherited the ophicleide orchestra parts, and since the tuba has about five times the resonance of an ophicleide, which had a wispy, anemic sound, you sometimes hear tubists in an orchestra overblowing. The worst thing a tuba player can do is dominate an ensemble, and the best thing he can do is blend and balance and affirm.

"The tuba is at the tonal bottom of the brass ladder. At the top is the trumpet, then comes the French horn, which is not French and should simply be called a horn. The trombone is next, and then the tuba. Each rung has its subdivisions. There are piccolo trumpets, F trumpets, cornets, B-flat trumpets, C trumpets, and bass trumpets. There are F tubas, E-flat tubas, CC tubas, and double-B-flat tubas. The breathing for singing is parallel to the breathing for brass instruments. One must have breath support, and breath support is being able to contain a full volume of air in your lungs without coughing or exhaling. Breath control—what you do with the air when you release it—is the key to artistic execution. But there can be no breath control without breath support. In one way, the tuba is the most comfortable of the brass instruments, because it has the largest mouthpiece. In another way, it is the most difficult, because one has to move so much air. It's extremely hard to play a C above middle C, and it's equally difficult at the low end of the instrument. You have to constantly clarify the tones down there. You can't just hope the right note will come out. A lot of tubists have no sense of control; they let their lips flop around inside the mouthpiece. The tuba has, after all, two main parts—one is flesh and the other metal. All the metal part can do is accommodate the flesh. If you play a beautiful phrase, the tuba will amplify it. If you play a bad one, the tuba will amplify it. One must learn to *practice*. The definition of practicing is when you go into a room by yourself with your instrument and make a lot of terrible sounds, because you're working out things as yet unrefined. You are not performing or even rehearsing. You are practicing.

"There are three reasons why the tuba still suffers a ridiculous image. One is the inept playing of many tubists. Another is the dreadful comic—in quotes—sounds tuba players are asked to make in the line of duty, and that includes the classical and jazz worlds. And still another is that the tuba solo repertory is so new. The horn had its own concerto in Mozart's time, but the tuba had to wait until Ralph Vaughan Williams produced his Concerto, in 1954. So when I first came to New York, in 1950, the only tuba solo with orchestra I knew was George Kleinsinger's 'Tubby the Tuba,' which was written in 1941. People have unthinkingly laughed at it, but there are many lovely things in that piece. We also had such treats as 'When Yuba Plays the Rhumba on the Tuba' and 'Asleep in the Deep' and 'Down in the Deep Cellar.' Since the late fifties, the tuba repertory has grown faster than any other instrument's. I want the tuba player to have an in-depth legacy to lean on. I want him to know he has roots. Any time I meet a composer I admire, I don't let up on him about writing a piece for the instrument until I get a positive answer—which may take as long as twelve years. The air that lets performers exist is created by composers, and you have to have plenty to survive. Hell, if Prokofieff and Stravinsky and Ravel and Schoenberg and Webern and Bartók and Berg and Tchaikovsky and Berlioz had each written a concerto for tuba, it would be a recognized solo instrument now and every orchestra would have a tuba section instead of one tuba, and we wouldn't have well over a hundred tubists applying for the tuba chair in the Baltimore Symphony, which happened not long ago.

"I went to Indiana in the fall of 1971. I replaced my friend and teacher William Bell, who had retired. I came over from the New England Conservatory, where I'd been helping Gunther Schuller. When he was made head of the Conservatory, in 1967, he asked me to be his assistant. He had never run a music school, or any school, and he needed some armor. The place was in dreadful shape, spiritually and financially, and I at least had had some administrative experience along the way in bookkeeping, personnel, and managing. I learned something about teaching at the Conservatory, and I'm still learning. I don't just teach the tuba to my students; I teach them life, if you will. I tell each student he only has one musician to compete with the rest of his days—himself. And I try to make him understand the ethical responsibilities of being a professional musician. Musicians have been laughed at and considered loony long enough. If a student of mine plays badly at our weekly meeting, I want to know why. Is he sick? Is one of his family sick? Is it drugs, love—what? I get to the problem while it's festering. So we indulge one another, and eventually we have a feeling of partnership. Which is what made the first Octubafest possible. I wanted my freshmen and my recent graduates to get acquainted musically and socially. And I wanted everyone to perform a solo. We had five recitals—one each night for five nights. Forty-six major works for the tuba were played. On Sunday, when the Octuba was over, we had the Fest—a party that went on out at my farm, which has eighty acres and a lot of animals, from twelve noon until the next morning. This year, we had fifty-three Octubafests on as many campuses. I want, eventually, to expand and coördinate these so that a composer can have a première in a hundred or more places at once. Why should a première be heard only by the occupants of a single hall?

"I graduated from high school in Marionville, Missouri, in 1947, and I got a summer job playing tuba with the King Brothers Circus. This came about through Homer Lee, who taught music at my school and had got me started on the sousaphone. He looked like Ichabod Crane and was a retired circus band-leader. When the word reached our

Methodist preacher that I was joining a circus, he came out to the house and Mother received him in the parlor. 'That boy will be destroyed if he works in a circus,' he said to my mother. 'Circuses are full of the wicked and degenerate. He will be lost.' Tears came to my mother's eyes, and she said, 'You don't have much faith in Harvey, do you, Reverend? Well, I do,' and she showed him the door. Homer Lee found me a York BB-flat tuba, and Mother made me a modesty cover for it out of a blanket. The taxi man in town was going to visit a relative in Syracuse, and he said he'd drop me off in Binghamton. From there, I got a bus to Waterbury, Connecticut, where the circus was. I was met at the station by a trumpet player with one leg and a drummer who was afflicted in such a way that he couldn't close his mouth. The leader of the band, A. Lee Hinckley, kept a wad of tobacco in each cheek when he played. I'll admit the sight of those three made the Reverend's words pass through my mind. Also, I'd never been farther from home than a Boy Scout camp, so the food, which I couldn't eat, and the three-inch mattresses and no sheets took me by surprise. But eventually I got on top of things and began enjoying myself in all ways. They paid me five dollars extra a week to drive a truck and carry the blues, which is what the planks used for bleacher seats were called. There were no maps to get from location to location; you just followed arrows marked on phone poles and trees. One time, the brakes on my truck failed. I rocketed down a long hill, and what saved me was jamming the gears into compound low when it ran out of steam halfway up the next hill. After nine weeks, I left to go to the University of Missouri, where I had a scholarship.

"I was miserable there. I slept in a rickety bunk in a basement with a local boy, and I carried my room and board by raking leaves and stoking the furnace and cleaning the house. I had eighteen hours of subjects and worked nights at the School of Music. Then a telegram came from Merle Evans, the leader of the band with Ringling Brothers and Barnum & Bailey Circus. He offered me a job on tuba at eighty-seven fifty a week, and I was to go to Sarasota right away if I was interested. Well, I called Homer Lee, and he said immediately, 'Harvey, get down there with Merle.' They knew each other, and, of course, to Homer, Ringling Brothers was it. So I closed up at the university and went.

"It was some different from the King Brothers. Ringling had a thousand or so on the payroll. The band traveled in its own railroad car, with a porter and a kitchen and clean sheets every week. Merle had his own stateroom. Johnny Evans, who was no relation to Merle, was the tuba player, and sitting beside him every day was a free lesson. I think the greatest compliment I ever received was after I'd been with the band six months and one of the trumpet players said, 'Harvey, I couldn't tell whether it was you or Johnny playing tonight.' The drummer was Red Floyd. He had a lined, pruny face, and looked like Old Man Time. I think he had played in New Orleans. He had a crippled left arm, but he was an extraordinary musician. He played all the mallet instruments, and he did a beautiful snare-drum roll with one hand by holding two sticks parallel in that hand like extra fingers and seesawing them so fast they became a blur. When we played New York, Sidney Catlett would spend all afternoon at the Garden watching Red, and then ask him to autograph a pair of his sticks. One of the trumpet players was Al Hiltensmith. He was red-faced and had a waxed mustache, and he'd been with John Philip Sousa. He chewed ginger root all day, and lived for the trip his first glass of beer gave him when it hit his ginger mouth. One of the band's jobs was to give the alarms. We played 'Stars and Stripes Forever' when a disaster impended, like the Midwestern storms that lifted the great center poles in the big top four feet off the ground. And we played the 'Twelfth Street Rag' when a high-wire act fell, which I saw happen one night. The tune was a signal for the clowns to come out and distract the audience. My first year, we hit every state in the Union. I stayed at the old Forrest Hotel, on West Forty-ninth Street, when we were in New York, and between shows I didn't know what else to do, so I'd play duets with the sounds in the pipes in my room. During my second visit to New York, I met Bill Bell, who was the tubist with the Philharmonic. Johnny Evans didn't come on the trip, and Bill Bell replaced him at the Garden. I got to know him, and I fell in love with the man. He was a marvelous human being, who had a grace and distinction I've never run across in anyone else.

"I stayed with Ringling Brothers until 1950, and I'd be there still—I consider it my career—if I hadn't got a wire from Bill Bell when we were playing in Los Angeles. It said I had a full scholarship at Juilliard. This was the second time someone had grabbed my shoulders and turned me around and given me a push in the direction I was supposed to go in. I went to New York, and I was in Juilliard off and on for four years. I lived for a while in Bill Bell's studio, on 121st Street, in a back room with a man named Eric Hauser. He was a fine horn player, or had been. But he'd become alcoholic, and Bill took care of him. He'd sit on his bed and criticize everything I played. I learned that way, and I learned from playing duets with Bill Bell and by going to rehearsals and record dates with him. In 1953, I joined the Sauter-Finegan band for about six months. It knocked me out with its fantastic arrangements and crazy instrumentation. Then I started with the New York City Opera and the New York City Ballet, and, except for a fine two-year stint in the U.S. Army Field Band, I stayed on the New York scene, working twenty-four hours a day, until I joined Gunther Schuller in Boston and had to commute to keep my hand in.

"My first method book—and without question the best—was a hymnal. I'd play out of that for hours. Even now, I have my students use a hymnal, so they can learn the effects of lyrics on music.

"The tuba is not accepted in jazz the way I'd like it to be, so it will be a great day when the first Clark Terry of the instrument comes along. They used the tuba in the early days before the string bass was adopted, and it reappeared in the Claude Thornhill band in the late forties, when Gil Evans was the arranger. Miles Davis had a tuba in his Nonet recordings in 1949 and 1950. I think he used Bill Barber. The finest jazz tubist is Rich Matteson, who has played with the Dukes of Dixieland and is on the faculty at North Texas State. I wish I had more opportunity to improvise. When I was with the Ballet in New York and doing the Conservatory gig, I'd sit in at Jimmy Ryan's sometimes before I took the plane back to Boston. But there doesn't seem to be time for things like that now, and improvisation comes a lot easier if you do it steadily. Jazz players grow and change like stones in a stream—from rubbing constantly against each other.

"I was born the tenth child of ten children on December 2, 1929, in Aurora, Missouri. I had six sisters and three brothers. My oldest brother was born in 1905 and didn't get married until 1949, and he was a second father to me. Another brother, Jesse, which was my father's name, died the year before I was born, and once in a while my parents would call me Jesse by mistake. My father came from a family of farmers. He was born in 1882, in Shelbyville, Tennessee, and his family moved to Missouri in 1887. He had four brothers and two sisters. Like many people during the Depression, my father did anything— plumbing, carpentry, electrical work, farming, barn-dance fiddling. He had a great sense of humor and a terrible temper. A couple of cows that belonged to a neighbor strayed into our yard once, and my father put them in the barn lot for safekeeping. The neighbor came by and saw the cows in the lot and accused my father of stealing them. My father went purple, and the neighbor jumped in his car and bowled out of the yard, but not before my father had thrown a hammer clean through his rear window. He used to tell us stories every night when we went to bed, and sometimes he was so tired he'd fall asleep in mid-sentence. On Saturdays, after we'd been to town, where they'd try to help people out of work by throwing free chickens from the upper windows of the courthouse, which used to bother me, he'd play the fiddle for us and we'd pop corn and eat apples from the cellar.

"My mother was—is—very tiny, very feminine, and very hardy. She was born in Marionville, Missouri, in 1888. Her father was a blacksmith. When she was four or five, he locked up his shop one day and nobody ever saw him again. My mother was married when she was seventeen, on New Year's Day, 1905. She handled the feeding and dressing of ten children without applause. She did her laundry with a scrub board, and she made her own soap. She didn't enjoy the benefits of plumbing and electricity until she was almost sixty. She baked bread every day, and in the spring she'd pick wild greens—lamb's-tongue and dandelion and poke and dock—and cook and can them. We all picked blackberries and hazelnuts and walnuts and gooseberries, which had to be stemmed on both ends. We'd have contests to see who could de-stem the most. I've never seen my mother raise her voice in anger. I've seen her show disappointment in her eyes and face, which is far more devastating than any words of anger. When we were little, she'd sit at table and wait until everyone had finished before she took anything—if, indeed, there was anything. Like many Southern country people, her favorite word is 'well,' but stretched out to several syllables. It's generally said in response to any kind of news. When I called her from New York to tell her that Carol and I were going to get married, she let loose a terrific 'Well,' paused, and said, 'There've been two deaths here.'

"All four of my father's brothers were farmers, and their land, together with my father's, was near their parents.' They had something like twelve hundred acres in all. But when the Depression came, my father had to give up his land. The primary reason was that although the farms were owned by his flesh and blood, each brother bought his own equipment instead of chipping in to buy common tractors and harvesters and the like. That pig-headedness wiped them out. After that, my father harvested wheat in Kansas and worked for the W.P.A., which, God knows, kept our part of the country going by allowing people their pride. From the time I was born until I was ten, we lived in nine different houses, which we called by their owners' names. The first was the Demond place, and the only thing I recall was nearly being flattened by a mad sow when I dropped my straw hat into her pen and went in after it. I started school at the Burney place, and I also plugged every last one of my father's acre of watermelons to see if they were ripe, and killed them all, which got my reputation for two whippings a day going. I was six when we moved to the Bacon place, and in time I had fourteen rabbit traps that I ran every morning, so we could have fried rabbit for breakfast and I could collect my eight cents a skin. I also went to a one-room schoolhouse and won all the ciphering matches, some of them against eighth-graders from other schools. At the Smith place, we raised beef and sheep, and I drove Aunt Sally from down the road to church in her horse and buggy. We finally settled in a three-room house near Marionville. We bought it for $800—a hundred down and five dollars a month. This was the house I finished growing up in, and it was the house my father made something livable out of. He picked it up off the ground four feet and put a foundation under it. He put in a furnace and plumbing. He wired the house. He added a wing with three rooms, and he built a shed and a garage. And he did it all with used wood—which added to the work, because you had to find it first. And he planted a lot of trees, which are huge now.

"I did what I could to help out financially. I picked strawberries and apples and peaches for a penny a box. I took care of a neighbor's mule for fifty cents a month, and I worked in a grocery store on Saturdays. I worked with the movie projectionist Saturday nights, and ran the projector myself when I was eleven. I worked at the funeral home, where I mowed the lawn and unpacked caskets and went with the town ambulance when a deceased had to be picked up. I was given a lot of responsibility early."

Phillips's five recitals at Carnegie Hall could be considered a bust. They were, with the exception of the last one, poorly attended (there was no Phillips money for publicity), and they were given just two short notices in the *Times*, neither of which said anything about Phillips's extraordinary playing. On top of that, *Newsweek* ran a "funny" tuba piece and interview with Phillips in conjunction with the series, and that almost unhinged him. Nonetheless, there was a triumphant air about the concerts. Most tubas engulf their players, but Phillips holds his so that it looks no bigger than a flügelhorn or a French horn. He rests it easily on his right thigh, its bell up, and he secures it with his left hand, which he flops casually over the top tubing. He plays effortlessly, and the only indication that he is maintaining his breath support is the sharp, windy intakes of air at the end of his capacious phrases. He is a magisterial yet invariably accessible player. At slow tempos, his timbre is soft and smoky and somewhat like Tommy Dorsey's trombone, which is held in high esteem by brass men. At greater speeds, his playing hardens in a muscular, singing way, but he is never brittle. His tone is light and direct, whether he is hitting a C above middle C or whether he is rummaging in the huge lower register—an area where the finest tubist can grope, his candle blown out by his own bearish notes. Phillips's sound is unique. His tuba suggests a graceful trombone, or a horn minus its nasal quality, or a baritone saxophone of the most velvet persuasion. His technique is astonishing. His arpeggios are glassy and clean, the alarming intervals he sometimes has to play are deft and exact, and his staccato passages are cream. Most of the composers who write for him purposely include passages of such complexity that it is possible no other tubist could maneuver them.

The final recital was suitably climactic, and it came to its peak in Alec Wilder's 1959 Sonata for Tuba and Piano. The first and third movements are slow and unabashedly lyrical, and Phillips made poems of them. His tone was soft and daringly burred, and his vibrato barely moved. He slid from phrase to phrase with the warmth and spontaneity of improvisation. He made Wilder's melodies—so close to his beautiful popular ones—three-dimensional. Afterward, Wilder expressed his pleasure in Phillips's rendition indirectly by saying that although Phillips had told him the series had been a financial disaster, he felt the tuba had been furthered in New York. "Anyway, I'm not at all worried about him," Wilder went on. "I was in his hotel room before the concert, and I watched him wrap a package of sheet music to mail back to Indiana. You wouldn't believe the things he did with mere paper and twine, the tightness and neatness and finality of his wrapping, the *strongbox* look of the package when he was finished. The only way to open it when it gets there will be to blow it up."

How to Paint

JON SCHUELER AND MAGDA SALVESEN

Painters should live close to the sky—for light, for stimulation, for perspective. That, in many ways, is what the painter Jon Schueler does. He divides his year between New York and Mallaig, in Scotland. In New York, he and his wife, Magda Salvesen, live in a big white twelfth-story loft in the West Twenties. It has four exposures and a view that runs from Hoboken, in the west, to the Chrysler Building, in the northeast. The sky presses in at every window. In Mallaig, a small fishing village on the west coast of the Highlands, Schueler and Salvesen live in an old schoolhouse under the huge weatherswept Hebridean sky. Since his first visit to Mallaig, in the late fifties, he has ceaselessly painted its skies, and they have come to possess him. He has attempted to describe what he does, but emotion invariably wells up and his words grow dizzy. Here is part of a note he wrote for the catalogue of a one-man show held at the Whitney Museum in 1975: "From the claustrophobic terror of my studio I enter the unframed sky. There I find every passion, soaring to Death, as certain and as fleeting as the intimacy of a night mist . . . I fall in motionless silence across a high sky. I watch the light spread through the shadowed snow-cloud and the sea, and I recognize what I have always known and have come here to find: Not the Highlands, but a nameless place—unless North is a name. It is truly North. The sun and shadow and infinite sea, all of it the sky, vast and intimate . . ." John I. H. Baur wrote in the same Whitney catalogue:

> Jon Schueler has walked a difficult path between opposites. His paintings look abstract but are not. The character of the Scottish coast . . . speaks through these poetic canvases with remarkable clarity and exactness . . . And yet these are basically abstract pictures, not unrelated to the work of Mark Rothko or some of Clyfford Still's big canvases. They have that kind of largeness, mystery and power. . . . He risks more by deliberately exploring a narrow area where nothing is secure, where everything is changing, evanescent and evocative. We see his paintings one minute as clouds and sea and islands, the next as swirling arrangements of pure color and light.

The writer B. H. Friedman, another Schueler admirer, talked of him recently: "I first met Jon at a party in the fifties. Franz Kline was there, and I told him I had just bought a painting by a young painter named Jon Schueler. Kline introduced us, and we've been friends for thirty years. Jon has always looked at me as an orderly man, and I've always looked at him as a romantic. His interest in jazz, his love of women, his painting—all these things are highly romantic. And when I first knew him he was extremely good-looking—in a Peter O'Toole way. He is very loyal. He remained loyal to Clyfford Still, who had been a teacher of his, and Still was one of the most difficult people I've ever met—irascible and practically a John Bircher. Jon has never let politics get in his way, and he has always had a remarkably clear head on such matters. He understood what a terrible mistake we were making in Vietnam long before I or anyone I knew did. Unlike many painters, he is a careful reader and an astute critic. He has an amazingly large and diverse social circle. He loves meeting new people, and he always carries cards and a little address book and follows up in a nice way. He is a generous host. Once, he gave a party for a West African dance troupe, and I recall a guest's asking one of its members—they were all sophisticated French-speaking blacks—what tribe she was a member of and her replying, '*Je suis Pygmée.*' Jon is highly respected by other painters, but he has not had the success he should have had. He was a member of the second generation of Abstract Expressionists, and got caught between the first generation, of Rothko and Still and Pollock and Newman and Kline, and the third generation, of Rauschenberg and Warhol and Jasper Johns. The money came down on both sides of him. Countless people have admired the Schuelers I own and not known who he is."

Schueler's early sky paintings, dating from the late fifties, were bold and heavy and intense, and were done with strong, complex fingerlike strokes. They tended, in texture and weight, to be more earthen than ethereal. Since then, his sky paintings, some enormous, have moved back and forth between periods of subtlety and delicacy and periods of great strength. In the delicate ones, the fog or mist or clouds look as if they had been breathed onto the canvas. The mountains and islands float, the sea is blue light. Everything is lucent and gentle. A layer of light gray covers a darker gray, and under that is still another gray. Grays and blues and violets and off-whites rule these canvases. In his strong periods, his pictures are often full of reds and blacks and yellows; they are tumultuous and angry. Their images are noisy. They come up off the canvas. All his pictures appear to be bottomless. They are never still. They have a restlessness and fluidity that are further stirred by whatever light they hang in. A Schueler seen in the morning and at dusk is two different pictures.

The elevator to the Schueler-Salvesen loft opens into a wide hallway. At the right is Schueler's office, and across the hallway is his studio. To the left, the hallway passes a utility room, a bathroom, and a spacious open kitchen. Opposite the kitchen is a dining area, and beyond that a bedroom. The hallway ends in a big, light living room, and off the living room is Magda Salvesen's office. Schueler's paintings hang everywhere, and they are like windows in the walls. Schueler is thin and stooped and medium-sized. He stands out against the Arctic white of the loft. He has intense blue-gray eyes, overhanging eyebrows, and wild gray hair. A small, ruly beard balances his hair. His quiet voice camouflages the urgency behind everything he says. He has a bright, short laugh and a snaggletoothed smile. Magda Salvesen is slim and lithe; she appears taller than Schueler but isn't. She has a cloud of curly brown hair and a V-shaped face, lit by deep-brown eyes and a dazzling smile. She is quick. She runs from the living room to the kitchen to fix lunch, she runs to answer the intercom or telephone. She thinks and talks fast, and has a kind of stutter, in which whole words, rather than letters or syllables, jam together in their haste to get out. When she answers the telephone, she may say four "Hello"s in a row. She has a luxurious, stately contralto that seems to assuage the flow of her words. Sometimes the sound of her voice blots out her words. She loves to talk and so does Schueler, and here, in counterpoint, are their autobiographies:

Schueler

"I was born in Milwaukee, in 1916. I come from the German middle classes. My mother's father, Rudolf Haase, was born in this country and was in the furniture business. My father's father, Fred Schueler, came from Bern, but was German. The Schuelers had a printing company in Switzerland. Both grandfathers prospered and were moral, hard-working men. Grandfather Haase didn't miss a Monday Rotary Club lunch for fifty years. My father met my mother, Clara Haase, at a Masonic party. I see my childhood two ways. When I was in it, it looked like this: I lived for several years with my Uncle Fred Schueler and Aunt Marie, who was of Polish extraction and was a warm and giving sort of person. One day, walking along a path, I met the woman who would be my stepmother and to all intents and purposes my mother. Her name was Margaret Alice Vogt. My father had met her at Battle Creek Sanitarium, where she had been studying to be a dietitian. She was thirteen years younger than he was, and she was beautiful. There were always levels of combat between us, but she raised me in her way. When I was twelve, that childhood ended. I happened to overhear a maid talking about someone who had died when I was six months old, and I slowly understood that she was talking about my mother. I never told anyone what I'd heard. I never asked my father, and it became a kind of guilt-ridden secret.

When I was nineteen, my stepmother brought a shoebox down from the attic and gave it to me. It was full of my mother's effects—rings, letters, photographs. I burst into tears, and my stepmother was furious, and said, 'I did everything for you!' In San Francisco, after the war, I heard from the woman who had nursed me as a baby. She had probably saved my life. She told me that when she came to work for us I was suffering from rickets and malnutrition. It seems my mother was breast-feeding me, and because there was something wrong with her, her milk had no nutrition. My mother died—I still don't know why—and that nurse brought me back to health. She stayed on a couple of years, and one day, she told me, she said she was going for a ride with her brother and she never came back. I don't know exactly what happened, but I suspect things had gotten too intense and she wanted to marry my father, or vice versa. I tend to lose things, and by degrees I have lost everything in the box my stepmother gave me, with the result that my mother, vanished, looms larger than ever. The beat of my life has come out of her death and the mystery that surrounds it. My father could be hard, but he had integrity and he was fair. I came to have great affection for him. He never went beyond the eighth grade, and he was a self-made businessman. He had some problems during the Depression, but my stepmother kept him together. It was her saving pennies that enabled me to go to college. I asked my father once why he had always taken her side in our battles, and he said that the marriage would have broken up if he hadn't, and that in many ways she was a good woman. When he retired, they moved to Santa Monica; he planned to spend the rest of his days playing golf, which he loved and had tried to teach me. But he had a heart attack almost immediately and died. My stepmother is still out there, near my half brother and half sister.

"I had done well in school until puberty and the news about my mother hit me. Then I started going up and down like a teeter-totter. I went out for basketball in high school, but I wasn't any good, and I went out for track and became a miler, but I was never in any races, because no one else had a miler. I had worked one summer at J. C. Penney, selling ties and shirts, and when I graduated they asked me to stay on. That was pretty depressing. Then my stepmother gave me the money to enroll at the University of Wisconsin. It was a very liberal place, and I went a little crazy. I joined Alpha Delta Phi, which was the best drinking house on what may have been the best drinking campus in the country. But it's a good thing I cut loose, because I had been treated like a twelve-year-old at home. When I was in high school, I had to go to bed at eight-thirty, and all my clothes—terrible clothes—were chosen for me. I studied journalism at first, and ended up with a degree in economics. I was at loose ends after graduation until a girlfriend of mine released the dream in me of being a writer. She persuaded me to get my M.A. in English and become a teacher. I got my degree, and the summer of 1941 I went to the Bread Loaf School of English, in Vermont, paying my way by waiting on table.

"I didn't have any desire to be drafted, so I joined the Air Corps in September of 1941. I wanted to be a pilot, but they discovered an astigmatism in my right eye, and I ended up a navigator with the 303rd Bombardment Group, in Boise, Idaho. My pilot was a Jack Armstrong type named Billy Southworth. His father was the manager of the St. Louis Cardinals. We didn't get on too well at first—particularly after I had messed up on the way out on a training flight and he had said to me in plain hearing of the crew, 'I don't suppose you know where we are?' On the way back, I used dead reckoning and hit everything one hundred per cent, and that night he told me in the officers' club that I'd done a terrific job. We became great friends, and I was devastated when he was killed in an accident just before the end of the war. In November of 1942, we flew our B-17s to Newfoundland and from Newfoundland to Prestwick, Scotland. We were socked in eleven days in Newfoundland, and finally took off one night at twelve-thirty after being on alert since six that morning. We flew between layers of storm clouds, and we were tossed all over the sky. It was beautiful inside the plane, with the green lights on the instrument panel and the *ah-ah-ah-ah* of the great piston engines. Then, after a couple of hours, the stars came out, and I felt I could contain the universe. I discovered we were eighty-five miles off course. I corrected our heading, and we landed in Prestwick just forty seconds off our E.T.A. The next day, we flew down to Molesworth, sixty miles north of London, for three weeks of training, and after a two-day pass in London we started flying missions. We were one of the very first American bomber groups. We had no fighter-plane protection, and very little idea of what we were doing. We missed targets more often than we hit them, and the Jerries discovered very quickly that the B-17 was vulnerable from the front. We flew over France, then went into Germany. I flew nine missions. One of the worst was when we ran into hundred-mile-an-hour head winds coming home and were forced to fly at an airspeed of fifty or sixty miles an hour. The Germans were on top of us, and our planes were going down everywhere. I remember saying to myself, 'Please, God, get this terrible boredom over.' The creeping along and the endless destruction had turned into a kind of huge, deadly boredom. Around the time of my seventh or eighth mission, I got a terrible cold. Colds were an anathema, and we dreaded them. Nonetheless, I volunteered for a mission over Saint-Nazaire, and on the way back we were forced to go right down to the deck to avoid the flak and get away from the German fighters. I have never felt such excruciating pain as I did in my ears on our descent. After my ninth mission, I was made an assistant command navigator and was transferred to the VIII Bomber Command, in High Wycombe, west of London. I caught the mumps and went into a terrible depression, and after that I got chicken pox. They put me through narcosis treatment, which is supposed to stop anxiety from feeding on itself, and in the fall of 1943 they sent me home. I was discharged in February, 1944. Three-quarters of the people I had flown to England with had been killed. The day rarely goes by that I don't think of that."

Salvesen

"I was born in 1944 in Midlothian, about five miles from the center of Edinburgh. It was still countrified. We had two fields and a river and a garden. I was the fifth of six children—Kirsty (or Kirsteen), Ann, Katrina, Johnny, me, and Andrew. My given name is Magdalene. My father and his father were born in Scotland, but the Salvesens had come over from Norway in the nineteenth century. My father still spoke a thick Norwegian dialect, which he kept up for business purposes but never suggested we learn. We went to Mandal, in southern Norway, every other summer, and when we were eleven we were permitted to go up to the fishing hut my father had built in the hills. We stayed two or three weeks, and almost the only people we saw were occasional berrypickers and a farmer a couple of miles away who sold goat's milk. There were ponies and a lake, and we slept in a loft in narrow beds laid between the joists. My mother loved it. I have often wondered if she was fearful being so far from a doctor, but, if so, she never showed it. Her name was Eleanora Cameron. She was called Mora. She came from a Scottish naval family and grew up in genteel poverty. They moved from naval base to naval base, usually in England—it was a peripatetic life. My mother had a soft face and lovely hazel eyes, and had red hair when she was young. She had been beautiful, I think, but she didn't trust her looks at all. She was of that period when all women had permanents, and she would get to look so much prettier when her hair got loose and frizzy—then off she'd go to have it done up again. Mother was twenty-six when she got married. She thought it very old. She was ten years younger than my father, so by the time I was a teenager both parents were middle-aged. All my mother had ever wanted was to run a house and have six children, and she did it wonderfully well. She had worked in an AGA-stove showroom before she was married, but there was nothing in her that felt that a career was of the least importance. It was baffling to her that I wanted to go to university. She was afraid of intelligence, particularly in women. She did read biography, because she had a compassion for people, a great patience for people. Her life was the kind that touched those around her very deeply. My father's name was Harald. He was remote, but in his way he was a family man. He was proud of his peasant ancestry and proud of how far his family had come. He ended up in shipping, but he spent the First World War in the Army in India and Persia. He never lost that Army look of the straight back and the mustache and the neatly brushed hair. After the war, he went up to Oxford and got a first and stayed on as a don for three or four years, teaching economics. Lord Longford was one of his students, and so was Hugh Gaitskell, of whom he was very proud. My father was very Scottish. He was élitist, and it was never easy for him to talk to people of all sorts. Yet he was truly democratic, and if there had been a Social Democratic party he would have been a member. He believed you should take responsibility and think things out for yourself. He was wary of people who had inherited high positions and didn't live up to them, and he couldn't stand civil servants who didn't take their work seriously. I had always thought of him as domineering, but after he died, in 1970, the schedule at home went on just as before—breakfast at eight on weekdays and at a quarter to nine on Sundays, lunch at one, and dinner at seven-fifteen. My mother continued to arrange flowers and keep up her garden."

Schueler

"Before I'd left the States for England, I had married a girl named Jane Elton. She was a saucy little thing—very amusing, very sharp. She was a speech pathologist, and she taught riding in the afternoons. She was the second person who has saved my life. I had with great difficulty gotten permission to go off base and get married just before we shipped out, and because of that I missed a disastrous training flight—the plane I would have been on flew into a storm and crashed, and almost everybody was killed. When I got back to the States, Jane and I lived in New York for six months. She was getting a degree at Columbia, and I got a job with an industrial-research outfit. Jane liked jazz, and I had played a little piano in high school—mostly for noon dancing and with a trio I had. We started going to the clubs on Fifty-second Street. I met Oscar Pettiford, the great bassist, and we became close friends. Oscar had a ferocious temper that could flare up after a few drinks. He was part Indian and part black, and he felt the pressure of racism in the States terribly, and eventually he moved to Europe. I last saw him in Paris in 1958, and he died under mysterious circumstances two years later.

"In 1945, we moved to the San Fernando Valley, in Los Angeles. Anita O'Day lived down a little dirt road from us, and when Dizzy Gillespie brought the first bebop band to the West Coast I invited the band to dinner, and Dizzy went out and played on the lawn at two in the morning. It was glorious. My wife had started taking a night course in portrait painting, and I decided to join her, which didn't please her too much. Art had had no place in my life. Most of the students had had some training, but all I could do at first was look at the model. The teacher, David Lax, was aware of the first tremblings of Abstract Expressionism. He kept looking over my shoulder, and he made me aware of the vitality of art. I worked first in charcoal, then in oils. We moved up to San Francisco in 1947. I taught English at the University of San Francisco and went nights to the California School of Fine Arts. My marriage was breaking up, and I moved out. We had two girls—Jamie, born in 1944, and Joya, after Joya Sherrill, the Ellington vocalist, born in 1946. Jamie works in forestry in Oregon, and Joya lives in the Mojave Desert and works at Edwards Air Force Base. Their mother is dead. The California School of Fine Arts was a very exciting place. Richard Diebenkorn and David Park and Elmer Bischoff were teaching, and so were Rothko and Clyfford Still. Still was extraordinarily dynamic, and he turned the school upside down. He had come out from New York, bringing the early news of abstract art. Much of his talk was evangelical—the independence of the artist, the importance of truth in art, and so forth—and it was exactly what I wanted to hear. But he tended to talk in circles. You'd feel the poetry of it but be hard put to it to repeat what he'd said. He was very persuasive. If he wanted to, he could make you believe that all Renaissance painters were charlatans. He could be kind and supportive, and he could be very critical. He hated the academy, and he hated galleries and museums. He talked about New York in terms of combat. He played cat-and-mouse with the galleries and museums, and they would end up chasing him. In the late fifties, he was invited to do a one-man show in New York, and he refused. Instead, he had one at the Albright Gallery, in Buffalo, which meant that everyone had to go to Buffalo, and the show made even more noise than it would have in New York. Of course, opinionated people like Still are essentially fragile, or they wouldn't go to such lengths to overrule other people and prove their own strength. One day, Still brought in a portfolio of reproductions of late Turners. I looked at them, and suddenly I knew that that was what painting was—the way the paint was handled, the imagery of the sea and the sky. Still left the school in 1950 and went back to New York, and when he returned for a visit I had a long talk with him and decided to quit school and go to New York."

Salvesen

"All of us were sent away to boarding school. It had nothing to do with getting us out of the way—it was just done, that's all. I went to Prior's Field, in Surrey. I was very happy there, and I made a lot of good friends. But I haven't been very happy about it since. The school library was limited to the classics—the Trollopes, the Scotts, the Eliots, the Austens. We were allowed to bring only four books from home, so we read each other's books after we'd finished our own. We learned a limited amount very thoroughly—Shakespeare and Chaucer line by line. When I spent six months in Paris between Prior's Field and university, I would read Racine and Molière in the same way before going to see productions of them at the Comédie Française. We wrote papers about social mores in Hardy and about whether or not the Napoleonic Wars had any influence on Jane Austen's novels. We were never told anything about Maugham or Graham Greene or Evelyn Waugh or T. S. Eliot or Yeats. Yet we were supposed to be incredibly eclectic in the British way—debate any side of a question and be thoroughly convincing. I've since had a terrible reaction to the education at Prior's Field. I rarely read a book or go to a play that doesn't have to do with the twentieth century.

"I went on to the University of St. Andrews, across the Firth of Forth. It was sixty miles from Edinburgh, and you took a ferry to get to it. We had mostly lectures, and I think the teachers were bored. I took French and English and Latin and moral philosophy. I took a whole year of Anglo-Saxon, and I still know the reasons that 'mouse' turns to 'mice' in the plural. I was somewhat cowed by St. Andrews. That made me unadventuresome, and even more timid than I already was. What saved me was spending a year on scholarship at Sweet Briar College, in Virginia. The campus was lovely, and there were views of the Blue Ridge Mountains. It was very sheltered, and your morals were looked after. It was 'Now, girls, time to work' or 'Now, girls, we're going to the theatre in Charlottesville.' Sweet Briar stimulated me far more than St. Andrews. I was still terribly idealistic, and many of the teachers there were really involved in their subjects. And there was a steady infusion of outside culture, ranging from Peter, Paul, and Mary to Reinhold Niebuhr. There were also many ambitious, intelligent girls.

"I went to the University of London after St. Andrews and got my M.A. in the history of fine art. That was 1968. My mother was horrified.

She found it all very dangerous, and felt that the more educated I became the less likely I was to get married. So much education made you selfish and opinionated and bossy. My options when I graduated were getting a job as an assistant curator in a museum or teaching art at the college level. I went home and worked in a gallery in Edinburgh, hardly being paid. Then I got a job as an exhibitions officer with the Scottish Arts Council. They had a gallery in Edinburgh and one in Glasgow, and they put together all manner of exhibitions that travelled all over Scotland. I helped choose the exhibitions and supervised their hanging. It was a great challenge to arrive in a new town late in the afternoon and find all your paintings stacked against the walls of whatever hall, waiting for you to put them up. I had a Mini car, and I travelled up and down the country. It was a wonderful job."

Schueler

"At first, I lived in Clyfford Still's studio, on Cooper Square. It was on the top floor of a town house with elaborate bannisters. We had lunch together a lot, either at a cafeteria that became the first Five Spot or at McSorley's. My first studio was at Twelfth Street and Fourth Avenue. I was there a year, then moved around the corner. The first building had a little restaurant on the ground floor, which sent evil smells up the airshaft, and the second had a noisy union. Many of the painters in New York lived in my part of the village, and it was a tremendously exciting time. I continued seeing Still, and I met Barnett Newman and Franz Kline. I liked Kline immediately. He never got out of his painting clothes, and his studio was a mess. But he always had one beautiful thing on hand. Once when I went to visit him, there was a gleaming sink from Macy's sitting in the middle of everything. He'd sold a picture and bought it. And he loved cars. He had a Thunderbird, then a

Ferrari. I had taken up the bass in California, and I was still playing. I had a good beat, at least, and I sat in at places like the Village Vanguard. I studied with Lennie Tristano, who was the Clyfford Still of the piano. We'd play together after my lesson, and it would lift you into realms you had never been in before. But the bass was taking up too much time. I had to make a decision, and I did: no more bass playing. It was sad, because I probably had more fun doing that than anything else in my life.

"You could live for nothing in New York then. The Tuesday-night openings at the galleries provided free social gatherings, and most evenings I had dinner at the Cedar Street Tavern— or the Cedar Bar, as we called it. It was on University Place at Eighth Street, in a building now gone. The clientele was chiefly white-collar people and artists—groups that floated easily through each other's curves. It was a homely, nothing bar with wooden booths and very good spaghetti. Fridays, everybody went to the Club. It met on Eighth Street and in various lofts. There were panels and heavy discussions, and afterward we'd take up a collection and buy a bottle of whiskey. The generations of painters were all mixed up. Nobody had any money, so we were all together. That changed later, and you became uncomfortable being around an artist who was selling paintings for fifty thousand when you weren't selling any. Lofts were just coming in, and they were plentiful and cheap. Their high ceilings and great wall space were one of the reasons why the abstract painters began doing such big pictures. Also, there was the influence of the Mexican muralists of the thirties, like Diego Rivera. And the painters discovered they could go downtown to John Boyle's canvas shop and buy cotton duck for a couple of dollars a yard instead of linen for twenty. When I got to New York, I thought I was well on the way to becoming a good painter, but I was soon shattered. Nothing much happened until Philip Guston came by my studio and looked at my work and told Eleanor Ward, of the Stable Gallery, about it. The Stable was on Seventh Avenue. She gave me my first show, in 1954. Three years later, Leo Castelli opened a gallery, and I was his first one-man show. On the basis of that, I went to Scotland.

"In England during the war, I had met a lovely, slim-boned girl named Bunty Challis. She drove one of those big, boxy ambulances, and nothing rattled her. She had been to the Highlands, and she would talk about its mountains and skies in images that reached dream images of mine—even though she was not that articulate. I brought back to this country what she had told me, and it stayed with me. Then I happened to see *I Know Where I'm Going*, with Wendy Hiller and Roger Livesey, and that did it. I rented a car in Scotland and drove around the Highlands looking for a place to live and work. Someone told me about a fishing village on the west coast called Mallaig. It was monumental. I was moving into my world. I stayed in a small hotel owned by Archie MacLellan, who rents me the house I live in in Mallaig now. He took me out to a little bungalow set all by itself near the Sound of Sleat, and I rented it. There I was all alone at the end of the world and the winter coming on. I hate being alone, and I thought, How am I going to get through this? But I caulked the house up—'It's not fair to the wind,' the villagers said—and I did forty-five paintings. After that, I went down to Paris, and came home and had another show at Castelli and a show at Hirschl & Adler."

Salvesen

"I met Jon at the Demarco Gallery, in Edinburgh, in 1970. He was very American, very definite about what he wanted. I was amazed by his ways in comparison with our muted Scottish ways. The relationship developed extremely slowly at first. He moved up to Mallaig—he had been going there off and on for years—and when he came back he announced that he was moving into my apartment in Edinburgh. He wanted to do a piece of writing and persuaded me to let him use my study. I only half wanted him to move in, but I didn't have the guts to say no. He was like a bull in a china shop, and I never knew what he was going to do next. I didn't tell anybody. I had never fought with my family. I was utterly different from my mother and didn't want to be sucked into her way of thinking, but I didn't want to hurt her, either. I didn't lie. It was an absence of telling at first. Then I told her in bits. She was very upset when she understood. Finally, I made up my mind about Jon. In 1971, I left the Council and moved to Mallaig with him, but kept my apartment.

"Mallaig is not a pretty, old, decaying Highlands village. It's a fishing village, and ugly and busy. Huge refrigerator trucks come in on the winding, tiny roads all the way from Bremen and Copenhagen to pick up fish. The surroundings are beautiful. On the east coast of Scotland, you look out and there's nothing there but the North Sea. On the west coast, you look out at islands and straits and sounds, and the feeling is utterly different. From Mallaig you see the Sound of Sleat and the islands of Eigg and Rhum and Muck and the Isle of Skye. Every island has its own shape and look, and they make an extraordinary combination. The weather changes constantly, so it affects you. You never know whether it will rage or shine or snow. You are very much aware of nature in Mallaig. Man has made no impact at all. The land gives nothing, and the people squeeze a living from it. There is little social life and no gentry, but there is a middle class, made up of the headmaster, ministers, bankers, and some retirees. They live in private houses, and much of the rest of the housing is council housing. There is a certain social life in the streets, and when I first went there I would be invited to women's houses for elevenses. They would serve tea and cakes, and I would ask them back for tea and a coffee cake or a cranberry-nut cake—things that they had never had before and that I had learned about in America. We would exchange recipes. There are many, many children in Mallaig, so a Mallaig friend and I formed a day-care group. I also did a great deal of reading and took care of our dog and arranged trips for Jon and me to Spain and Morocco and Italy and America. Jon is a timid traveller, and I had always travelled. I also did a lot of work for him—not willingly, I admit. He wanted me to be in on everything he was doing. He thought it far more important that I work for him than do things for myself. I resented his self-centeredness. People like Jon are very sure of their direction. I respect distance between people, but Jon will suck anyone into his life, his drama. He revels in emotion. He lives by the rule that feeling anything is better than feeling nothing. Also that there is no need to put the lid on any emotion. Of course, there were compensations. He was very appreciative of what I did for him, and he shared everything with me. But in 1975 we split up. I went back to Edinburgh and attended a teachers' training college, and Jon went back to America. But we wrote to each other, and in 1976 I came over, and we were married in July. Since then, I've taught several years at the Day School, up on Fifth Avenue, which I loved but which was exhausting because I also had to keep up with Jon. I've done some public-school remedial teaching, and now I'm teaching English as a second language. We go to Mallaig almost every year, and we've been to China, and I've just finished editing Jon's autobiography, which is over a hundred thousand words long.

"I see life in New York in terms of Mallaig and Edinburgh. In Mallaig, our life is extremely simple. Almost everything is cut out of it. We go days without seeing people, and one engagement a week can press on us. We're terribly excited when we get back here, and we go to all the galleries and see our friends, and then we retreat and settle down. Keeping up with what's going on in New York is a week-to-week thing, as opposed to Edinburgh, where it's month-to-month. In New York, you do things scatteringly—you dart off, you do things by chance. New York is raw compared with Edinburgh, which has its little green parks and seems built for people. Edinburgh is a wonderful residential city. I loathe the suspicion New York arouses in me vis-à-vis other human beings. Edinburgh is genteel and has few excesses. So much about a city like New York is unvoiced, but it is those very unvoiced things that keep you away from other American cities, which lack *it*."

Schueler

"Around 1960, I got divorced from my second wife, Jody Todd. She had been married to the poet Ruthven Todd, and I had met her on Martha's Vineyard. She was a painter. We were married in 1956 and separated in 1957. She had come over to Mallaig to make hotcakes for me, and she hated it, and we plunged into hell. Then I went through a time when I seemed unable to resist getting married. I would meet someone, like her, ask her to marry me, watch the relationship deteriorate the minute the word 'marriage' was mentioned, get married, go through hell, and have the marriage annulled. This happened twice— with a young black dancer and with a cheery girl who had just come down from Boston. The sixties were a bad time all around. Pop Art was taking over, Abstract Expressionism wasn't selling, and painters were talking about nothing but money. I had two shows at the Stable. I taught at Yale. I visited Alastair Reid in Spain. I found a new loft, at Broadway and Twentieth. In 1967, I went to the Isle of Skye, and did a very important series of watercolors. They took me closer to Turner, whose secrets are in his watercolors. I sold my lease to my studio in New York and moved to Chester, Connecticut, and built a studio there.

Then I got an offer from the University of Illinois—a full professor-ship, tenure, and twenty thousand a year. They wanted a kind of spiri-tual leader. I was painting, but I was broke. I suffered the anguish of indecision, then signed on the dotted line. I taught a year and took a leave of absence. I tried to take another leave, and they said no, and that was that. I had been approached by a dealer in Edinburgh named Ricky Demarco, who wanted to give me a show. I went over in 1970, and I met Magda at his gallery. She was with her mother and some relatives, and they were on their way to *Blithe Spirit*, which is not my favorite play. But I wormed my way into the party and went. Magda is like none other. She is independent and self-contained and she never feels the need to explain. She kept disappearing over the horizon. I really had to pursue her, to court her. In 1973, I showed a hundred and fifty paintings in three working studios at the Edinburgh College of Art. I mounted them myself. I had tables and chairs and arranged for a light lunch. People could sit down and look at the pictures and take their time. The show lasted four weeks, and I sold a lot of paintings. Between 1974 and 1981, I showed in Minneapolis, at the Whitney, at the Cleveland, and in Chicago. Then, in 1981, I again had a marvellous experience in Edinburgh. I was invited by the Talbot Rice gallery to be part of the Edinburgh Festival. What I did was paint six rather large paintings—two were eighteen feet, three were fourteen feet, and the last was ten feet—in public over a period of a month. I worked in a large studio, and the pub-lic watched from a gallery. I had an eight-foot palette table on wheels. The paintings were meant to reflect one another and to be in a state of counterpoint yet to be true to themselves as single paintings. I was stimulated by all that canvas, by the idea of the whole thing, by the public.

"In Mallaig, I often paint at night. In New York, the kernel I strive for is nine in the morning to one in the afternoon, although there are many distractions in the city. Each day, the struggle to paint starts again. It's easy to talk a picture and very hard to paint one. I try to make the experience of light real. I make my hand think light. I try to get the organic quality of movement, of change. If you let your eye move up a blank white wall, that wall changes every second. There are a thousand whites. Change is constant. So is surprise. Once a canvas is finished, the paint is frozen there. Yet it has an inner life, and as day moves over it it changes and changes. Long ago, I decided to go through Abstract Expressionism and come out the other side. The abstract painters rejected everything, but I felt that all painters were my brothers. I started painting skies before I knew what I was doing. Now it is my odyssey."

Schueler's studio measures roughly sixty feet by forty feet, and has an eleven-foot ceiling. It takes up two-thirds of the loft—a ratio that, Schueler has said, "most artists demand of their nearest and dearest." One end faces north, and has five good-sized windows. Four large tables line the windows. The tables on either side are palette tables, and the middle ones are covered with tools. The south end of the studio is filled with paintings, many of them enormous. Some are stacked face to the wall and some are in racks. Two dozen aluminum studio lamps are fastened to metal rods hung from the ceiling. Schueler paints perhaps a hundred pictures a year. He prepares his canvases, which are made of cotton duck and are stretched by an assistant, with two coats of acrylic gesso, each sanded. He uses house-painters' two- to two-and-a-half-inch brushes, and one-and-a-half-inch brushes for final touches.

It is four o'clock on a cold afternoon, and Schueler is in his painting clothes—bluejeans, a tattered bluejean jacket, a blue turtleneck, and a bluejean hat. The sky is still blue, and the top of the Chrysler Building is silver white. Schueler drives two nails into the west wall and hangs a fresh canvas, measuring forty-four inches by sixty-five inches. Before he hangs it, he sprays the reverse side of a small dent in its lower right-hand corner with water to tighten the cotton duck. He drives another nail into the wall at the foot of the canvas to keep it steady, and steps back about twenty-five feet. He stares at the canvas a long time, moving from side to side. He walks to the palette table near the west wall, squeezes out some paint, and walks back to where he had been standing and stares again at the canvas. Then, moving quickly on a semicircular path, he goes to the table, picks up a brush, works its end in the paint, continues on to the canvas, leans forward, and makes a single, startling horizontal pale-blue pattern from the left edge to the middle of the canvas. The pattern vaguely suggests a flintlock pistol, its butt to the left. He squeezes out more paint and covers the pattern with a pale gray, enlarging its right end at the same time. He takes a new brush and works at the right end of the pattern again, making it still longer and softening its edges. He keeps his brush at a thirty-degree angle to the canvas, and he works fast, holding the brush between his thumb and fingers the way old-time drummers held their sticks. Many of his strokes go against the grain of the brush. Using a battleship gray, he places a roundish, windy figure above the original pattern, adding a separate daub at the left edge of the canvas. He softens these new patterns with pale gray. He inserts a large blue-gray patch at the lower right of the canvas, and stands back and looks at what he has done. He covers the new blue-gray with a darker gray, and stands away again, the brush hanging loose in his right hand. His stance is easy, his knees slightly bent. He goes back to the canvas and makes a blue-gray pattern at its top left, a cloud coming into a clear sky. He darkens the center of the original flintlock pattern with a purple-gray, and adds a whitish gray to its butt. The layers of paint float on the canvas. He puts a whitish blue on the new cloud pattern at the top, and places daubs of it in mid-right and upper right. A third of the canvas is filled with paint. The sky outside has darkened, and the studio has grown brighter. More whitish gray appears at the top of the picture and at the right of the original pattern. Schueler pedals backward like a quarter-back and stares a full minute at the canvas. He holds his brush in both hands in front of him—a cook about to drain a big saucepan. He adds blue-gray to the top pattern and down in the lower right, and enlarges the right section of the original pattern. Its outlines are no longer vis-ible. Gray goes into the center of the canvas and whitish gray along what was the bottom of the original pattern. He adds a blue swatch to the bottom of the painting and a narrow band along the underside of what was the flintlock. Blues and grays control the canvas. Schueler inserts a patch of violet in the top right quarter of the canvas. Then he stretches a more vivid violet across the bottom left and over a gray area at bottom right. His movements have got quicker, and the only sounds in the studio are his shoes and the soft *thrush-thrush-thrush* of his brush. He joins part of the top right section to the right end of the orig-inal pattern with a bold gray-white column. He picks up a small brush and puts dark gray over the bottom left corner and between the origi-nal pattern and the top of the canvas, so that a rough, heavy gray arc dominates it. It is dark outside: the last of the afternoon light has been sucked into the studio. He covers the right center of the painting with a pale-blue swatch, and walks back almost to the opposite wall. He moves forward and sits down in a chair and stares at the painting for several minutes, his face propped in the fork of his left hand. He goes to the palette table and back to the canvas and applies a whitish patch at the left center, near the heavy gray, and in the upper right corner, and sits down again. He gets up and closes a white area at the top of the canvas with pale violet, and another, at top left, with pale blue, and the canvas is filled. During the next ten or fifteen minutes, he makes dozens of tiny changes with a small brush: a whisper of violet below the dark-gray center; a touch of white-gray at the upper right and along one edge of the dark gray, which produces the first hard edge in the picture; a very light coat of gray over a patch of blue at the upper right; a little staring white near the gray center. He softens the center by rubbing it with a cloth, then with two fingers. He adds a little blue to the top left corner and some pale gray to the far right. He puts down his brush and backpedals into the studio and stands still. There, suddenly, is the picture. It is an abstraction of a cloudy sky, and at the same time it is a cloudy sky. We are looking up into the sky, or perhaps we are in the sky looking down through clouds at still blue water. No matter where we move in the painting, the painting moves. Schueler is apparently finished. He clears his throat and says "Well!" and laughs. "It's that time of adjustment. I could go on until the whole picture was repainted, but I'll wait and see how it looks in the morning." An hour and five minutes has passed since he put the first blue on the canvas.